"Dancing On Broken Legs: Journey of a D.I.V.A."

Dancing on Broken Legs: Journey of a D.I.V.A.

Copyright© 2017 by Dr. Barbara Young

All rights reserved

All Scripture quotations, unless otherwise indicated, are taken from the NIV/KJV Parallel Bible, Copyright© 2002 by Zondervan and the Holy Bible New International Version®, Copyright© 1973, 1978, 1984 by International Bible Society, Used by permission of Zondervan. All rights reserved.

Printed in the United States

1st Printing, 2017

ISBN-978-1-938116-95-7

ISBN-978-1-938116-96-4

TFS Publishing Company

31600 Railroad Canyon Road, Suite I

Canyon Lake, CA 92587

Tel: (714) 794-9747

Fax: 951.244.4778

E-mail: www.transformationforsuccess.com/dancingonbrokenlegs

Website: www.transformationforsuccess.com

To
All of the
Reedy Women

Happy Reading

Dr. Barbara
7/15/2017

You all have "S"!
Know your heads!

"Dancing On Broken Legs: Journey of a D.I.V.A."

Dr. Barbara Young

TFS Publishing Company

Canyon Lake, California

DEDICATION

Special heartfelt Memories to my dearly departed
beloved:

Grandmother Lula Hammond

Mom Minister Idessa Dossett

Dad Jonothon Sanford

Aunt Ernestine Kiano

Sisters (deceased) Paristine Wofford & Alma Lee
Garrett

Brothers (deceased) James Dossett & William E.
Dossett

SPECIAL DEDICATION

My husband, Douglas Charles Young, who loved me
and was the wind beneath my sails and demonstrated
this each day of our 37 years of marriage.

My daughter, Danielle Lelah Humphrey, whose light,
laughter, and love filled me with joy each day for 30
years.

To my children: Crystal Bouldin and Hammond Bouldin
who loved me and gave me such inspiration to write
this book! I love you both dearly!

CELEBRATIONS for
Dancing On Broken Legs:
Journey of a D.I.V.A
by Dr. Barbara Young

"I worked with Barbara for several years on the nonprofit board of Leadership America, a unique leadership development program for women. Barbara exemplifies the very best in leadership qualities having "walked the talk" and been an inspiring example for women for almost 40 years. Having overcome many obstacles in her life, I am sure this book will provide incredible examples and personal stories that will be not only interesting but also insightful. She has reinvented herself whenever the times or needs have changed such that she is just as relevant today as she has been throughout the years. I don't know many women who can match her resilience, faith, and success. She is   awesome and so will *"Dancing On Broken Legs: Journey of a D.I.V.A."* be awesome!"

~ Lana Porter, President, Ameritech, Inc.

"Dr. Young has so much to impart to the world and this book will allow many people to gain insight, knowledge and skills who otherwise would not have the opportunity. This is brilliant!"

~ Lena Kennedy, President, LLK Associates
Executive Director, Women's Health Conference and Expo

"To achieve what is possible starts with positive thinking. Dr. Young has not only inspired me to think positively, but has moved me into taking action on projects that I previously only dreamed of. Dr. Young is very passionate about helping others to envision the triumphs and successes that lie ahead in the face of adversity. It is no wonder that Dr. Young has transformed and empowered so many women in her long career. I highly recommend you read *"Dancing on Broken Legs, Journey of a D.I.V.A."* It will move you to start taking action in achieving your dreams."

~ Caitlin Chen, Bank Manager

"Dancing on Broken Legs: Journey of a D.I.V.A." goes right to the heart. Dr. Barbara Young is my friend, confident, and teacher. I have learned so much from her life and the lessons she has brought forth to share with others. She has served admirably as the lead instructor on leadership development and public policy for the Los Angeles African American Women's Public Policy Institute (LAAAWPPI). She teaches that a true leader must look inward, take the lead from the Higher Power, and be authentic and true to themselves. In that way an individual can truly inspire, help and lead others. She has finally put her life lessons in this long-awaited book. Hallelujah!"

~ Joy Atkinson, Executive Director, LAAAWPPI

"I have known Dr. Barbara Young for well over 25 years. While the world knows her as a leader and authority on higher education, life empowerment, and issues related to women and families, I know her as a friend, mentor and trusted advisor. Dr. Young is a dynamic speaker, author and visionary thought leader who has taught, mentored encouraged, and inspired thousands of people. I count myself as one of those. Her book, *"Dancing on Broken Legs: Journey of a D.I.VA."* is truly a "gift" of inspiration to the world!"

~ Aristide J. Collins, Higher Education Administrator

"There are very few women I know who are as charismatic and loving in addition to being a transformational healer as Dr. Barbara Young. She is a blessing to all whose life she touches. I had the good fortune of meeting her at a book-writing seminar a few years ago and we experienced an instant connection! She gives of herself above and beyond the norm to all that have the good fortune of any contact whether it is personally or thru her shows or seminars. Her passion, compassion, and enthusiasm are infectious. I know that her struggles throughout life, that are revealed in her writing and coaching, has transformed her into the incredible leader that we know today. We all have a lot to learn from Dr Young and I'm honored to call her my friend. *Dancing On Broken Legs: Journey of a D.I.V.A.*" will embrace your mind and heart and is a must read for all!"

~ Barry Rose, MD, Chief of Orthopedic Surgery

"Author of The Cutting Edge of Compassion"

"Dr. Barbara Young's spiritual strength is contagious. She is a coach's coach. I met Barbara over 25 years ago and we became sisters in every way. As Board Chair of Leadership America, Dr. Barbara invited me to join and guided me in matters of diplomacy and "war"--as she does in this book. Ours has been a legendary friendship and sisterhood, bound together by her sincere interest in me becoming my best self. *Dancing on Broken Legs: Journey of a D.I.V.A.*" is a book of wisdom, fortitude and discipline. It reads wonderfully--as if Dr. Barbara is speaking directly to you. In this book, Barbara gives hope to all who journey through these pages."

~ Pamela Freeman Fobbs, JD

66th President, Auxiliary to the National Medical Association

"This beautifully written book tugs at your heart and entices your mind. Read about the inspirational and very personal journey of one mighty woman of God. She lives, learns, and encourages you to be all you can be!"

~ Marcia M. Wade, M.P.A.

Vice President, Human Resources

"Dancing on Broken Legs: Journey of a DIVA," is a must read to motivate the readers to take charge of their lives in the most positive way." Within these pages, you will find the Lord's mission for the life of the author, Dr. Barbara Young, who has won over many challenges and the person I have known most of my adult life. We have walked together; we have traveled together; and we have cried together over our loved ones who have made their transition. I have been honored to provide her with an opportunity to travel abroad with me to visit other areas of the world. Open and outgoing, she has made lasting impressions on those she has come in contact with and offered them advice on how to improve their circumstances spiritually and in their civil lives.

~ Dr. Diane E. Watson,
Ambassador/Congresswoman Emeritus, 33rd District

"If you are interested in personal and professional renewal, you will be inspired and motivated by Dr. Young's book, *"Dancing on Broken Legs: Journey of a D.I.V.A."* This book will help you share and understand someone else's struggle; it will give you strategies and successes with overcoming; it takes you down a path of empowerment that overpowers defeaters' attitudes of feeling victimized by emotional inner and outer conflicts.

~ Coco York, Musician, Music Therapist and Behavior Specialist

"Dr. Barbara Young ends the introduction to her wonderful book with a quote from Henry James stating, "It's time to start living the life you have imagined." Barbara has done this in spades and this book is a richly inspiring testament to the amazing courage, intelligence and, above all else, heart of a truly remarkable woman who has accomplished a true rarity...she has walked the talk. Sharing her life with this reader has left me equally inspired and humbled by what is possible when one makes up their mind that this is MY life to be lived."

~ Blaine Bartlett, #1 International Best Selling Author &
Founder of the Institute for Compassionate Capitalism

"Dr. Barbara. Young, is a Presidential. Bronze, Visionary, Business Member with the Chamber of. Commerce. She is an exceptional individual, and well versed in the merits of the world. She possesses some very unique qualities. Her amazing footprints can be seen everywhere, from the West Coast of California to the Eastern seaboard in and around our Nations Capitol of Washington. D C. and well beyond the U.S, as she has traveled extensively throughout the world. I know that everyone will undoubtedly benefit tremendously from not having only read this God-sent well-written book, *"Dancing on Broken Legs: Journey of a D.I.V.A.,"* but also having the grand opportunities to make her acquaintance I truly feel their lives will be empowered and be richly emboldened to accomplish anything one sets his or her mind to do in life."

~ MC Townsend, President, Black Chamber of Commerce, SFV

"Dancing on Broken Legs: Journey of a D.I.V.A." is a consequential read for women and men of all ages and backgrounds. Her book is inspiring, touching and forthright! She will provoke and embolden your thinking and self-reflection as she shares her story and provides us with practical examples of how we, like she, can use and follow God's word to help effectively confront and overcome the personal and professional challenges we experience."

~ Rhoda Posey, Mentee and Friend

"Dr. Barbara Young is a 'gifted' woman of God with a story to tell. God has not only blessed her with beauty, but wisdom, grace, and favor. She has a way of seeing past a situation and prophetically uncovering the root cause of physical and emotional pain. If you spend any time with her, you will know she changes lives. She is a Transformation Coach, Author, Pianist, Singer, Speaker, Teacher and Mother, I can't wait to read her book, *Dancing on Broken Legs: Journey of a D.I.V.A."* because I know my life will be even more enhanced!"

~ Bonnie Winfrey, CEO/Chief Media Strategist
Kailen & Kyler Enterprises

"Dr. Barbara Young's life has been and still is a marvelous inspiration to all who choose to listen and learn. Her life story is a journey of emotions from joy and laughter to devastation and outrage to heartbreak and mourning to triumph and victory-all with the underlying theme of continually pushing forward one step and one day at a time. I have gained insight into my own life experiences from hers and I'm confident you will as well in her book, *Dancing on Broken Legs: Journey of a D.I.V.A.*"

~ Millena Gay, Producer, Actress, Entrepreneur

"Powerful! Inspirational! Refreshing! Dr. Young is open and honest and she holds nothing back. This book is a must read!"

~ Karen Abercrombie, Actress, The War Room

"Dr. Barbara Young is an extraordinary Woman of God who has reached her full potential walking in her destiny. It is marvelous in the way that she has been used by God to inspire, strengthen and encourage many lives, students, and parents educationally and spiritually. This book is an inspiration to all of us from her personal walk with God to show off our own dance and display wisdom in our lives and the lives of others."

~ Dr. Kenneth L. Preston, MS, MBA, DBA
Project Engineer/Team Lead/Technical Lead Engr/CAM

"Dr. B epitomizes Maya Angelo's quote 'My mission in life is not merely to survive, but to thrive; and to do so with some passion, some compassion, some humor, and some style" thanks for sharing your story of triumph! Much love from your fans in Africa."

~ Rose Musau, Founder and CEO,
Preferred Personnel Africa Ltd.

Dancing on Broken Legs
Table of Contents

Dancing on Broken Legs
Table of Contents

FOREWORD

Every once in a while, God throws caution to the wind and creates something wonderful. He presses courage with kindness, love with fierce conviction, laughter with tears of compassion and rolls out one of his very own.

On that same road, the Lord seeks out those that will listen, trust him enough to follow his lead and allow him to design their journey. He found that in Dr. Barbara Young.

In this book, "***Dancing on Broken Legs: Journey of a D.I.V.A.*"**, Dr. Barbara Young shares her story through a series of real-life vignettes. She doesn't hold back! Dr. Young leaves it all on the page giving the reader a candid view of the good, the bad and the miraculous.

This book represents the next best thing to a personal sit-down with this dynamic engaging individual. You can expect to laugh, cry, gasp and experience a series of "ah ha" moments. All this while learning how God divinely directs and creates the paths of our lives. As an author, Dr. Barbara Young is transparent, humorous and entertaining.

The millennials will say she's "bout it-bout it". The "seasoned" people will pause and call her amazing. Those in the middle will call her beloved sister, but ALL will call her blessed.

Enjoy your read as you are ushered into "*Dancing on Broken Legs*: *Journey of a D.I.V.A.*"

~ Althea Ledford, Editor

E The Magazine for Todays Female Executive

ACKNOWLEDGEMENTS

This book has been in progress for almost ten years. My heart is grateful and thankful for my many sister friends and supporters who encouraged me to write this book. I could not name all the people that have had a special impact on my life and an immeasurable influence on me to write the book, *"Dancing on Broken Legs: Journey of a D.I.V.A."* as the list is very long and wide.

To my beloved husband, Douglas Charles Young. I think of you every day and thank you for thirty -eight years of a wonderful marriage. Thank God for sending you in my life. I know that you are up there with God cheering me on. I miss you.

Most importantly to Crystal and Hammond. I am so glad that God blessed me to be your mother. Since the day you both were born, and every day since, you both have been a blessing to me, even though there were some tough times. It was laughter, love and prayer that kept us close together over the years. Being your mother has been the best part of my life. I respect and admire you both. This book is dedicated to you, and your wonderful and light-hearted sister, Danielle who will always be in our hearts. I know that you each are destined for greatness as you walk down your paths with God on your sides! You are both world-changers.

There are, however many people who were very influential along the journey of my walk, and have heard many of my stories over the years in my motivational talks. To those people, individually and collectively, thank you. I am very blessed to have been touched by all of you.

Special thanks to my friend and traveling companion for years, Congresswoman Diane Watson, who was always there for me and I will always value her friendship and support over the years. I became her "sister" in spirit, light and love.

To my cousin, Coco York, whom I have always admired and is a great singer and performer, thank you for being there for me in "good" times and in the "difficult" ones. You have been my champion every step of the way and I love you for it.

Thanks to my friend, Rose Musau, who invited me to speak in Kenya and became my most ardent fan, and who showcased me in Kenya for many years.

Thanks especially to some of my fantastic friends and supporters over the years; Mollie and the late Jim Ware, Howie DeLane, Sumatra Kirkland, Donnie Machen, Carol Barbee, Frances Chavis, Norma Warren, Ty Melvin, the late Rev. Leon Ralph, all of whom were always cheering and encouraging me through the tough times and the good times.

A special thanks to my newer friends, Ruthie Ledezma, Debbie Minor, Joy Sterling, Robbie Motter, Desiree Doubrox, Blaine Bartlett, Bill Walsh, Barry Rose, and Joanna Padgett, who are both noted authors whom I met at a writer's workshop and have since been my "cheering" section.

Thanks to Joel Comm, my New York best-selling author friend, for reaching out to me and inviting me to his writer's workshop where I learned invaluable insights and information on how to write a book. Your wisdom, generosity, and infectious enthusiasm showed no boundaries. You were truly an inspiration.

To Lorene Wood, I especially thank you for giving me your wise counsel, encouragement, honest feedback and useful criticism over the years, even when dealing with so much in your life. You and David were, and continue to be my champions.

Althea Ledford, you were more than a friend. You were with me every step of the way with your almost daily emotional and spiritual support, enthusiasm, encouragement, and authentic friendship. Thank you for your support in the design of the book cover and all the tips on how to organize the book for publishing.

I also want to acknowledge Steve Ragland, who is such a talented photographer for his beautiful cover photo of me. He was such a dear heart to shoot the photos in my home for my convenience.

Thanks to Melissa, Victoria, Andrea and Rhoda for sharing their expertise and talents in the initial reading, input and typing of the manuscript for this book.

Thank you, Joan Wakeland, and Nancy Mueller for your feedback as the first readers of my manuscript. I will always remember your inspiring words.

Thanks to my long-time friends and ardent supporters for well over twenty years, Dr. Denard and Pamela Fobbs who were always there for me. Thank you, Pam, for the final editing of this book.

Thank you, Bishop Blake, and Lady Mae for your love and support over the years, and how you both knew when to reach out to me during my darkest moments. I am blessed to know you as my Bishop and First Lady.

Finally thanks to all the participants in my Personal Best Success Life Growth Seminars in California, Kenya, Senegal, Tanzania, and the many countries I toured on the continent of Africa, and to the wonderful women who learned and grew in my Life Growth Seminars, Leadership workshops and Policy Development sessions locally and nationally over these past years. Thank you for your transparency in sharing your challenges, dreams and successes with me. I am deeply honored to have been a part of your lives and you in mine!

Special thanks to Hammond G. Bouldin, web-master, designer, and text coordinator for his incredible work in helping to produce this book.

Thanks to Crystal for her constant encouragement, persistence and support to get the book finished.

PREFACE

Dr. Barbara Young was awarded in 2016 the Lifetime Achievement Award of Excellence by President Barak Obama. She is an on-line TV/Radio Talk Show personality, a national and internationally sought -after in-demand dynamic speaker and consultant on leadership development and transformation success. She is an entrepreneur, educator, life coach, author, and transformation success expert.

Dr. Young also has well over 40 years of experience in education as a re-careered senior level higher education administrator and as a university adjunct professor. She has served on a number of city, state and national boards in leadership roles. She has received numerous awards from state, local officials, national legislators, and community organizations for her expertise and work in leadership, public policy, teaching, consulting, radio broadcasting, and success coaching.

For the past 20 years, Dr. Young has also worked as a consultant with academic institutions, city municipalities, health care agencies and non-profits, community organizations, churches, and corporate professionals and world leaders from Fortune 400 and 500 companies. She is passionate, high energy, spiritual and dynamic. Dr. Young excites, inspires, educates, empowers, and helps individuals and organizations to use transformational principles personally and professionally for success that she designed from a "holistic" perspective.

Her view is radically unique. More importantly, she offers success solutions and results that work. Many call her the dynamic Dr. "B" after experiencing many of her motivational and inspirational talks and powerful seminars. Dr. Young is the powerful "Dr. B" who has inspired some of the most successful people across the world to action who has transformed their lives today. She is passionate and her mission is to "transform the lives of millions of individuals, one step at a time," so that they too can step into their destinies and impact the world!

Dr. Young has a BA degree in Social Psychology, a MA in Counseling Education and a Ed.D in Administrative Leadership and Organizational Behavior from the University of Southern California (USC). She also has an "honorary" Doctorate of Theology from the Next Dimension University.

For more Information:

www.transformationforsuccess.com

INTRODUCTION

If you have picked up this book, I know for many of you, this has been a long wait. Many individuals, women and men over the years have asked me to write this book.

The idea of writing this book came to me the night my youngest daughter, Danielle, died at age 30 from the complications of diabetes in 1998. After nine days on life support I made the decision to let her die peacefully and go to be with God. This was possibly one of the harshest trials I have ever had to face.... the loss of a child. The title of this book, *"Dancing on Broken Legs: Journey of a D.I.V.A."* came to me early that next morning and it has resonated with me for all these years.

I was strongly motivated to write this book in 2006. I was scheduled to travel on one of my speaking tours in the continent of Africa. In anticipation of the book being written, I developed invitation cards for the book stating it would be released that fall. I shared with many audiences, and ladies completed the cards in large numbers.

However, I did not follow up with the book. Something within me kept telling me that it was not the time, and when the time was right that I would bring the book to life. That time is now!

This book shares how my life's disappointments were turned into stepping-stones to lead to my future destiny. I did not, however, think it would take 30 years in the making.

I was born in a small town of Muskogee, Oklahoma, the eldest of six children, happy, joyful, and always I am told, with full of energy. I had a strong feeling from the time I was age six or even earlier that God had chosen me to be a vessel. I went to a private school at age three, only to have first challenge at age 6. The school closed and I had to attend public school. Against all odds, and due to my persistence, I was admitted to public school at age 6 in the third grade, and graduated high school with top honors at age 15. In short, I was admitted to college at age 15, pregnant at age 17, married with my mother's permission, and with much shame, regretfully left college.

At age 19, with now two babies nineteen months apart, my husband left me with four fifty-cent pieces and disappeared. I had two small children, no food in the home, no job, no rent money and with a deserted husband, I ended up with no place to live.

At age 20, I stated and wrote down in my journal, that I wanted to "make a difference in the world."

In reality, I did not know how, where, or when. It was a journey of trials, setbacks, saboteurs, haters, insufferable bosses, disappointments in relationships and some triumphs that I finally began to look "up" and not "out" to realize that there had been a clear destiny path for me since childhood.

I share with complete transparency and authenticity of how I struggled and navigated life's teachable moments, learning sometimes by default, but later putting in action the success strategies and principles I learned as I traveled with many bumps in the road on my personal, and spiritual transformational journey.

God had a plan for me, and finally after many years in what I call the "wilderness experiences," and in total obedience to His will for my life, I embarked on a new journey of love and service with a purpose to transform the lives of men and women. However, the purpose did not come   without first extensive training for it. There was a plan and purpose for me, and it took almost 30 years in the making.

From the outside looking in, I am aware that most people see me today as the successful, attractive, dynamic super woman. After working on my internal self for many years, and going through a "desert" experience for twelve years, I realized that I was in training for a future job so vast that I could not imagine it. Oh, how I was perplexed for many years as to how this would happen when every circumstance around me seemed to be saying you are a "failure," and people were continually "putting me down," and criticisms were a constant.

However, in spite of numerous setbacks, I was blessed to continue my educational journey at age 36, receiving B.A and MA degrees and a doctorate at age 51. I have been fortunate to travel extensively as a motivational speaker and transformational success expert and consultant, sharing my story and the principles I learned giving messages of hope and encouragement to women and men throughout the world and the Continent of Africa. Moreover, I have had the opportunity to meet and share these principles with great leaders and famous individuals all over the world. I never dreamed that I would be living the life I am experiencing today.

I had an outrageous love affair for thirty-seven years with my third husband, and the love and support of wonderful children from a previous marriage whom I raised mostly as a single parent, and with whom I still experience a steady state of love, happiness, and balance.

If you are ready to learn the success principles on how to be a D.I.V.A. (Divinely Inspired, Victorious with Authority), then this book is a must read. D.I.V.A. is how God described me in 2006, "the D.I.V.A. who kept on dancing in spite of insufferable bosses, jealousy, sister friends who betrayed me, heart issues with relationships, emotional and abusive husbands, serious family issues and a leaky self esteem.

There were many challenges that occurred during the writing of this book; the sudden death of my mother, my favorite Aunt, my youngest brother, and my wonderful, loving husband who was the "wind beneath my wings. Douglas was diagnosed with dementia and thus this book was on hold. After seven years of caring for him, he died in October 2015.

It has been an amazing journey that I will share in this book. I spent 37 years in higher education, working my way up the career ladder from secretary to a college president, to a senior level position in a corporate educational headquarters, while working concurrently as an adjunct college professor. I initiated a number of innovative programs for high school and college students; I became a motivational speaker, traveling extensively sharing a message of hope and change. I honed my craft as a leader and was appointed to a number of national boards, and I learned my lessons well. I am a Godly woman, tall, and educated. I am talented; I am a leader, I am self-confident and courageous. I became character-driven rather than personality-driven. I learned to sharpen my skills, be patient, to grow and to incubate. I self examined periodically for cancer of the "soul" and "spirit" that I call (complaining, criticism, bitterness, unforgiveness, contemptuous behavior, envy and resentment).

I took a great leap of faith in 1977 and took a chance on life with God as my Captain and Program Director. Working on my inner self, growing and developing spiritually, yet remaining true to myself became a full-time job. I discovered that I, and I, alone could choose to be great or follow the road of mediocrity. I chose to walk the path to greatness. My personal victories, as well as the challenges and lessons learned with spiritual insights of wisdom have all helped me become the woman I am today. I am honored and constantly in awe in how God has blessed me to share my story to help many individuals, especially women around the world. Today, I am a top media personality and am CEO of my own on-line TV network.

As I have aged, of course, there have been more struggles, tests, mountaintop and valley experiences that I have overcome using the spiritual success principles I learned. I have been blessed in my travels to meet and be surrounded by numerous inspiring women and men champions in my life. They have consistently encouraged me to write this book, and with all of your support, the dream to write this book is now a reality and I am delighted to share it with you.

Reading these vignettes that are not in chronological order, you will find laughter, sadness, and joy and learn most of all that life is a choice and, as Eleanor Roosevelt stated, *"We are the sum total of the choices we make in life."* You choose the road you travel, you choose the God—the Creator you serve, and you choose right from wrong. I strongly encourage you to highlight any of the principles that I shared in this book that may resonate with you.

Truly I have become a D.I.V.A. (divinely inspired victorious with authority) and you, too can choose to be a D.I.V.A.

"It's time to start living the life you have imagined."
~ Henry James

Dr. Barbara Young
Canyon Lake, California

Chapter 1
The Journey Begins

I was born in the small town of Muskogee, Oklahoma with a population of 64,000 souls. I was the eldest of six children and we were called stair-step children. There were three girls, 19 months apart, and my three brothers, who were three and four years apart. My father was a hard-working man and worked two jobs, one at the local Veterans Hospital as a hospital orderly and on Saturdays he owed a shoeshine stand in a downtown barbershop.

My mother was a stay at-home mom who took in sewing for neighbors on a part-time basis. She was loving, but a staunch disciplinarian, a neat housekeeper, who was always tidy, and made us do chores, and clean her floors on our hands and knees, careful not to get her sideboards dirty. I learned how to cook at age seven and loved it. I began cooking for the family at age nine. By the time, I was 13, I had taken over cooking many of the dinners in the household for a family of eight. I was creative and became familiar with spices and herbs to use in the food that I cooked. Everyone loved my cooking and we ate our dinners together around the table every evening, and I recall we always had dessert that my mother would make. My father was always present and on time for dinner and we all, including my mother catered to him.

We were a happy family, with a church-going mother who took us to Sunday school, and as we grew older, we attended BTU, (Baptist Training Union) on Sunday evenings, and vacation bible school at all denominations during the summer. My mother instilled Christian values in my sisters and brothers and me, however, our dad only attended church on Easter and holidays. We were kept busy as children, but we had plenty time to play outdoors. My mother was always smartly dressed when we when out shopping, to church or to visit her friends. As the eldest, I was held responsible for the behavior of my younger brothers and sisters when she had to run errands or leave the home with my dad. I often state these experiences were my first lessons in the development of my leadership skills and being held accountable.

I was a bubbly, engaging child and always heard the sounds of music in my ears. I use to pretend that I was playing a piano in the window-sill's of my house,

2

and I was always singing. Life was good and I was happy.

I had a little dog-named Rex, and a red wagon, and each day, I would wander down the street in my mother's high-heeled shoes with my little dog in the wagon. When I got tired, I would take off the shoes, leave them there in the street and return home. Often times, I would have strong reprimands for this, but I would continue to wander every other day in her shoes.

One day, I wandered away from home in her shoes again, and I realized I had gone a bit farther away from home. I saw a little grassy knoll, and Rex and I ran over to the lawn and laid down on the grass. I had kicked my mother's high-heeled shoes off while running and as I lay looking up into the sky, I felt a little sleepy and I heard a voice from the sky say to me, "one day you will grow up and help many people." I got scared, jumped up, grabbed Rex, placed him in my red wagon and ran home, forgetting my mother's shoes.

When I got home out of breath, my mother met me at the door, looked at my feet and said, "Where are my shoes?" She had an angry look on her face and I knew I was in for a strong lecture or worse later, like not being able to play outside for a day. I never told my mother about the voice and what was said to me on the grassy knoll that day because not only did she restrict me from playing outside for a day, but two days. I was really sad because I loved to play outdoors.

Yet, I still would oftentimes sneak out in my mother's high heel shoes and roam and wander, but always remembering to bring them back home. As grew, I always felt there was something that I had to do, and it did trouble me from time to time, but as life went on, I soon forgot about that voice on the grass that day.

I read vociferously each day; it was as if I could not get enough of reading. I loved books, and read everything I could get my hands on. My mother was always after me about "having my head stuck in a book." I loved to draw, and I played with paper dolls until I was almost 12 years of age. I did not think that unusual until my younger sisters began to taunt me about playing with dolls at that age.

Principle Learned: _I felt special growing up and I just knew I had a destiny to fulfill at an early age and dreamed about it._

Scriptural Reference: _Jeremiah 1:5 "Before I formed you in the womb, I knew you; before you were born, I consecrated you; I have appointed you a prophet to the nations."_

Chapter 2

The Lessons

I went to a private school at age three. How I got there was interesting. Two female school teachers who lived across the street from where we lived, frequently saw me outside my home playing freely in the yard with one end of a long rope tied around my waist and the other end to a tree. One day, they asked my mother, "Why did she have me tied to a tree with a long rope?" My mother stated that I had a habit of wandering out of the yard and down the block. She was afraid something would happen to me and this was the only way she could keep me confined in the yard, while she was doing chores in the house and taking care of my baby sister.

After learning more about me from my mother, they asked if I would be able to handle attending a private school. They explained to my mother that they had started a school on the outskirts of town and needed students to fill the seats or they would lose their funding. They agreed to pay the expenses and my mother quickly accepted. She thought it would be a good way to keep me occupied as she was pregnant again and taking care of my sister who was nine months younger. Thus, I entered school at the age of three, and I always say it was because I was "potty-trained."

At age four, my mother and I were visiting a friend who lived across the street and she had an upright piano. I saw that piano and I got excited. I went over to the piano and began fingering the keys one at a time picking out the song that I had heard in my head. Incidentally, it was, "Mary had a little Lamb." The neighbor was both shocked and impressed. She turned to my mother and strongly admonished her to make a way to have me take piano lessons as she surmised that I had a natural ear for music, but would be limited with my talents, if I did not learn to read music.

So, a few years later, at age six I began music lessons, with another neighbor who also lived across the street. She was an accomplished classical musician and a noted piano teacher in the town. However, during my lessons as I would play pieces from Bach and Beethoven, I would improvise, and my piano teacher would always strike my fingers because that was a "no-no." I later learned that these were the "old" masters and you absolutely did not improvise on their music. I did, however continue to take piano lessons for years. I simply loved to play the piano and improvise. A few years later, one of my Aunts gave my mother the money to purchase a piano for me. I loved to this piano and I would play for hours and compose songs.

My siblings would complain about my practicing every day and the noise I was making, and as we grew older, they would pay me a nickel to stop practicing. These were fond memories I have of growing up. Since that time, I have had a piano in my home in what ever city I have lived.

Principle Learned: *It was my early training and recognition by my family and others of the gifts I had been given.*

Scriptural Reference: *Luke 12:48 "...Much is required from those to whom much is given, for their responsibility is greater"*

Chapter 3
Secrets of The Sacred Family

Secrets, someone has said, there are *"secrets"* in every family. Some secrets are kept forever locked away. My secret, kept for many years, became a turning point in my life in two occurrences. I had grown up being the eldest of six children, however, I was always the "odd" one in the family. I did not look like my brothers and sisters; I had different color hair, different skin color, and I was taunted and teased by them because of the differences in our appearances. I would question my mother, but she would off scoff at my questions and be very vague.

When I entered high school, two of the teachers remarked that I looked exactly like my dad. I was puzzled, because I bore no resemblance to my dad or mother. I went home and questioned my mother, and she replied, "Those teachers do not know what they are talking about." But later in the evening, I overheard my mother and father arguing, and I heard my name. I was indeed curious and began to wonder about my appearance and why I did not look like any of my siblings or my mother and father.

However, as time passed by I did not ask my mother any more questions, but pondered in my heart, "what was going on?" I continued to pursue my studies and get good grades in school; I took French and loved it. As I advanced in school, I read books copiously; I loved practicing my clarinet and French. I played my piano every day which was comforting, until my sisters and brothers would complain about the noise. I would also spend a lot of time drawing my own comics. I had grown particularly fond of drawing cartoons and I would spend hours doing it.

One day when I was 14 years of age and in the 11th grade, my mother received a telephone call that my grandmother was very ill in Berkeley, California. My mother was advised to come to Berkeley as the entire family was called to gather at her bedside, because they feared she would not live throughout the week. My mother feverishly packed, told my father, this was an emergency situation, took off in a day or so and left all of us six children in the care of my father.

My sister, brothers and me went pretty wild, playing outside until almost dark, and as my father was pretty laid back, he let us play outdoors for a long time. One evening, as it was just getting dark, and I went into the house to get a glass of water. My father cornered me in the kitchen, dragged me into his bedroom, and threw me on the bed, where he pulled up my dress, pulled down my underwear, and attempted to rape me. I was so scared, and struggling and screaming at the top of my lungs for him to stop when the telephone rang. The telephone kept ringing and ringing as if it would never stop. I was crying, "Daddy stop, why are you doing this?" and I kept fighting and screaming as he kept trying to force himself on me.

He was startled, and as the telephone kept ringing and ringing, he released me and ran to the phone, where I could hear my mother screaming, "Where the heck were you? I have six children at home and someone surely should pick up the phone this time of night." She told him her mother had rallied and that she would be leaving and coming home the next day. I ran outside and started calling my brothers and sisters to come into the house and that Mom was on the phone.

This was a turning point for me as I thought in horror that my own father had attempted to rape and hurt me. I was in shock and when my mother returned, I was afraid to tell her what had happened. I thought she would not believe me because he had been such a loving husband to her and as a father outwardly he had never exhibited any unseemly behavior towards my siblings or me. He acted the next day as if nothing had ever happened.

My entire personality began to change. Given the outgoing personality I was gifted with, I became very quiet, subdued and withdrawn. Even my teachers noticed a change in me and inquired if something was wrong. I would always respond that I was okay. I would stare in space during class time and wonder why this had happened to me, and what was it all about. I thought, "How could a father do this to his own child?"

I tried to rationalize it out in my mind. I kept thinking I was only 14 years old, tall for my age, and very underdeveloped. I was 5 ft. 8 inches with a size nine shoe, which was the bane of my existence. I was teased constantly because of my height and shoe size. I walked around somewhat for days and weeks in a fog. I did not want to be around my girl friends. I could not sleep at night. I was jumpy and easily moved to tears.

From that point on, I kept a small knife under my pillow as I slept in an enclosed-in sun porch which ordinarily I was so proud of because I had my own space and did not have to share it with my other sisters, as we were only a year apart. But this became my secret for 35 years. I was 14 years old and lived in perpetual fear of my Dad for almost two years. I became aloof, distant and stayed to myself and from everyone in the house. I stuck to my chores and books and was now in the 11th grade.

I slept with a flashlight under the covers to read at night, as my mother would make us turn all the lights out at night. I would keep asking myself how could a father do this to his daughter. And, my soul was not at rest for years after this incident. A secret such as this can fester in childhood and years   later; I learned this could result in a dysfunctional adult.

I managed to graduate from high school with honors and a 4.00 GPA at fifteen, making the National Honor Society with acceptances and scholarships to several universities. However, with much nudging from my aunt, who was attending UC Berkeley and getting her Public Health Nursing Degree at the time, she convinced my mother to allow me to attend Berkeley and that she would watch over me. My dad was not pleased at all and very upset about me moving away and kept insisting that I go to another local university where I could come home on weekends. I had overheard them talking about it and my mother was beginning to be persuaded and have reservations about me leaving home and going so far away at my young age.

I managed to call my aunt, share with her the conversations going on in my household and she assured me she would take care of it. To this day, I am not sure what happened between my aunt, my grandmother and my mother, but she was finally convinced that I would be safe living in the home with my grandmother and aunt while attending college. She stood against my dad forbidding me to leave home. As the time approached for me to leave for college, I needed new clothes and I wanted to work to help pay for them.

That summer, after graduation, I got a job as a housekeeper for a wealthy Caucasian woman in town. I was impressed with her home because among other things, it had a very large library and I was fascinated at seeing so many books. She found me one day marveling at her books, and when she found out I loved to read and that I was going off to college at age 15, she made a bargain with me. She agreed to pay me the regular salary for a maid, but she wanted me to bake her a cake once a week and read to her once a day from a book that I selected.

We would chat and have great discussions about the books I had read to her. She would talk with me as an adult and she inspired me to study hard and get good grades when I got to college and finish my education. She would always say she saw "greatness" in me and that one day I would do great work with people. Further, I could take any book home to read during the evenings as long as I returned them. I was a fast reader and so thirsty to read through as many books as I could from this massive library and most of all, I began to travel other worlds.

I worked for her for about a month when she finally had to hire a maid to clean her home. However, we stayed in touch and remained friends until I left for college. I never knew after that summer what happened to her, but will always remember her kindness and the encouragement given to me.

I soon found another job working as a waitress in a Greek restaurant downtown for the remaining summer months. The owner pointed out he had never had a *colored* girl working in his restaurant. He made it clear, however, that if any of his customers complained about me, he would have to let me go. However, to his and my amazement, not one of the customers complained and I was so happy to get the small sum of money he paid each week, because I got plenty of tips from the customers.

I was on a roll and beginning to feel my old self; I was saving for a wardrobe trunk to pack my clothes to go to UC Berkeley. Each week I would give the money I earned to my mother to hold in a mid-sized jewelry box she kept in her bedroom. In July, the time has come for me to purchase the wardrobe trunk as I was departing my hometown in two weeks. I was excited and could hardly wait to leave.

My mother had been sewing every day that summer to make some of the clothes I would need for college. The day arrived for us to go downtown to purchase the wardrobe trunk we had previously looked at that was located in a second-hand store. Luckily, it was still there and when she reached for the jewelry box in her large bag, she discovered there was no money in the box. She was embarrassed in front of the store clerk, and realized that my father had probably taken the money as it had always been kept in her bureau drawer. I was crying and could not stop.

When we got home, she confronted him and he stated, "Barbara needs to go to a university (and he named one 60 miles away) where she can come home every weekend." I knew then that my only out was to call my aunt, ask for money to purchase the trunk and leave that town. I called my aunt that evening, with my mother's permission and explained the situation. My aunt willingly sent the money needed for me to purchase the trunk and my bus ticket to Berkeley, however, I made up my mind, I would never ever go back home. I left several weeks later. But the hatred for this man was something I held for thirty-five years and I was finally able to forgive him with the help of God. I literally wept face down for two weeks to release all of the pain, hurt, bitterness, disappointment and disillusionment I had experienced.

Principle Learned: *Bad things happen to "good" people. However, for me to grow to become whole, forgiveness was a choice; it was up to me. I had to choose, let go and let God. Resentment and bitterness is poison to the soul, spirit and physical body.*

Scriptural Reference: *Matthew 6:14-15 "For if you forgive other people when they sin against you, your heavenly Father will also forgive you. But if you do not forgive others their sins, your Father will not forgive our sin!"*

Chapter 4

The College Adventure

I left Oklahoma on a grand adventure to Berkeley, California on a bright, sunny day in August. It was on a Continental Trail Ways Bus. I boarded and sat in the back that was designated the *colored* section. It was my first time sitting on a seat in the back of a bus. I was very frightened as I had never been anywhere by myself. There were two sailors in seats behind me who were going to Treasure Island in San Francisco. They were very friendly, and struck up a conversation with me. We chatted and they found out that I was going to UC Berkeley to college, and they were so glad for me; both stated they had to look out for me and they became very protective of me for the entire trip.

When we had stops, they were always looking to see that I was safe, had food and water. I felt as though God had sent me these angels to watch over me. After a long ride on the bus and when I reached my destination, my sailor friends sent me off with cheerful goodbyes and well wishes. I arrived at the bus station in Oakland, California. It was overwhelming to me. The building was huge to me, and as I walked through the station in my new suit I had sewn for the trip, I finally saw my Aunt, who was smiling and extending her hand to me. I felt welcomed and loved.

I recall from the age of 7, my awareness and appreciation of the mentors in my life (mostly female) had been and still is one of the most important factors in the development of my self-esteem, my sense of responsibility, my drive and my feelings about success and personal empowerment. My aunt reinforced these feelings in me as well as my grandmother, my teachers and my counselors, who were all African American.

Parenthetically, one of the critical factors in my transformation journey was my relationship with God and understanding at an early age that I was special and unique and I had a great job to do, albeit I did not know what that job was.

Settling in with my grandmother and my aunt to get ready for school at UC Berkeley, I soon discovered that it was not going to be an easy journey, in that college tuition was raised that fall to $60.00 for a semester. As it was then going to be a financial struggle for my aunt and grandmother with the increased fee, they informed me that I was not going to be able to enter UC Berkeley as had been planned.

My aunt explained that a new community college was opening that fall in Oakland and that there was a possibility I could attend for a few years and then transfer to UC Berkeley. This news was devastating to me that I had to now attend a community college before attending UC Berkeley which was not what I had envisioned.

In my heart, I just literally gave up and in a desperate moment, confided to my Aunt the experience with my father. I begged her not to tell my grandmother. However, a few weeks later, I received a letter from my mother informing me that the man who had raised me was not my father. This was as much information as she gave me.

I felt somewhat comforted, but I was very angry at the way my life was going. I was smart, frustrated, and felt betrayed in that I had come to Berkeley anticipating a life at a college campus of my choice. Then I found that I was unable to go to a college that I was accepted to at age 15. Finally, a way was made for me to attend college.

I was so excited to be on campus, I met so many people from all over the world, and never realizing that there were only two African American women that I met on campus. There were many Africans from the

19

continent of Africa. However, I soon adjusted to the diversity and blended in with campus life. Classes were extremely large, and in a year or so, I met a young man from France that changed my life. I was only 16 and he lived up the street from me, had seen me walking down the street after school. He had inquired of a friend who I was. The friend called me and asked if this young man could call me, to which I agreed. He and I chatted over the phone and he sounded very nice. He then asked me for a date to take me for an ice cream soda. I agreed and when he showed up at my door to pick me up, I was shocked because he was so very handsome, and he spoke French.

My grandmother was very approving because he was well dressed, and very handsome. I also became enamored of this tall, handsome man. He was a former basketball player with a team in France, and was just returning home to his parents, and after a brief courtship, at age 17, I found myself pregnant.

My aunt was furious and gave me three alternatives, one, to have the baby and give it away to her brother and sister-in-law and go back to college, two, she could perform a safe abortion as she was a registered nurse, and three, I could get married to the young man.

However, I knew she was sorely disappointed in me and did not want me to literally throw away my opportunity for a college degree. She kept pressing me for an answer, and soon I had to make a decision on the choices she offered me. Not wanting to abort my child or give the child away to an Uncle and Aunt I did not like, I made the decision to marry my handsome boyfriend that was putting pressure on me for marriage.

My mother had to give permission for me to get married at that age and I knew I was a disappointment to my entire family. I walked down the aisle with a man that I did not know very well, much less loved. I turned 18 that November, and gave birth to a baby girl in January of the next year, and did not return to college as I had planned.

It was a marriage with many deficits from the start; when my first child, a girl was 10 months old, I found myself pregnant a second time. With the birth of a son, my husband's family celebrated, as they wanted their son to have an heir to continue the family name.

Yet, I knew in my heart that this marriage was doomed to failure. My husband was not ready to take on the responsibilities of fatherhood, much less be a husband. He was young, a drinker, and wanted to womanize, party and spend money. He was also spoiled by his parents, and did not want to work.

Hence, my college adventure lasted a short while and for many years I felt an empty space in my .

heart, as it was truly my desire to attend and complete my education. However, I knew one day, I would finish what had been borne in my spirit

_____

Principle Learned: *Happiness like unhappiness is a proactive choice. We are free to choose our responses to any situation. The choice is ours. We are really the sum total of the choices we make; the ball is always in our court.*

Scriptural Reference: *Psalm 37:39 – "But the salvation of the righteous is of the Lord, He is their strength in the time of trouble."*

Chapter 5

My Struggle Comes In Trios

After three years of marriage, my husband came home and decided he no longer wanted to be married. He left me with two children and four fifty-cent pieces. I was heartbroken with tears streaming down my face. I did not know what to do. I had been waiting all day for him to come home from work, as it was his payday and we had agreed to go shopping for food that evening. I had no food in the house, and was giving my eight-month old baby evaporated milk and water all day, when he should have had whole milk. I was desperate but something within me knew that I would be victorious no matter what. I became very calm as both children were crying as though they knew something was awry.

I immediately called his parents, who came to the rescue with food and milk, and they were very disappointed in their son. They stated they would admonish him and encourage him to come back and take care of his responsibilities. This, he never did, and I was left on my own to care for my two children with no money, and no job. I called my mother who stated she could not help as she was having challenges on her own with my stepfather and his drinking. She shared tearfully that she did not have the funds to help me and was sorry for my situation and suggested that I reach out to her mother.

Adding to my plight, a few days later, a man from the water company showed up at my door to turn the water off because the bill had not been paid for months. When he saw me with one child clinging to my skirt and another in my arms crying, he stated, where's your husband? I explained to him what had happened. He looked at me and said, "Ma'am I cannot turn your water off with two helpless small children in the house. You need water for them and you need to be able to flush the toilets." I felt something inside me leap with hope. As a matter of record, my water stayed on through the entire time I stayed there, which however, was short-lived.

The next week, the owner of the duplex came to me and stated the rent was due and I shared I was not able to pay the rent. She was very sympathetic, and stated she understood my plight, but that she was a widow and this rent was her only income. She asked if there was anyone who could loan me the $65.00 that was due. I told her my mother was unable to do so, and

I did not get in touch with my in-laws as they had literally abandoned me as well. Somehow, I would try to get the funds.

In a few days, after much demanding from the landlord about the rent and how if I could not pay, she needed to rent to other tenants, I knew I had to leave the premises, and I had nowhere to go. I called and asked my grandmother who lived a few blocks away, and given I had lived there while I was attending college, I was certain she would say, "Yes". To my amazement, she said "No." I was hurt, feeling alone and rejected, with no place to live. I was frightened and felt that I would be homeless with two small children to care for and where could I go? However, God intervened on my behalf, and a day later to my amazement, I discovered that one of my Uncles had come to town and he came to visit me.

He explained he was staying with my grandmother. When I shared with him my circumstances and that I had no place to live, he stated he would speak to his mother. He later shared that he has spoken to my grandmother and found out that she was adamant that I could not come live with her and my two small children under any circumstances. She did not want to have two small children running around in her home, destroying her plants, and playing with toys everywhere.

There was no compassion for me and my little ones.

I knew in my heart that my grandmother loved me. I had fond memories of her taking care of me when I was a small child, teaching me how to cook my first batch of cornbread on a crate box in her kitchen. However, I could not understand at 19 with two small children and a vanished husband, that my grandmother had said I could not come with my two children and live with her.

My uncle intervened on my behalf to his mother. She reluctantly agreed to let me stay, but only for a short period of time. The condition was that I had to live on a cot in a hallway as she had rented out one of the three bedrooms to a renter.

Every night he had to pass by my cot in the hallway to enter his bedroom. Many nights I lay awake wondering how had I come to this — a cot in my grandmother's house, which was uncomfortable, and my children on a pallet in her bedroom. I would lie awake at night and pray that one day I would do better than sleep on an uncomfortable cot in a hallway, single, afraid, lonely, and with two small children to care for.

I knew in my heart that somehow that life would get better for me one day. I found out many years later that my uncle, who had left after a month in her home, had threatened never to speak to her or call her "mother" again if she refused to allow me and my children to live with her until I could do better and get on my feet.

Principle Learned: *God Intervenes on our behalf with people, even our family members, yet our responsibility is to keep loving them, and to trust and have faith in Him!*

Scriptural Reference: *Romans 8:28: "And we know that God causes all things to work together for good to those who love God to those who are the called according to His purpose."*

Chapter 6
Miracles Do Happen
for them that Seek

Given the circumstances I knew I had to find a job and an apartment to live with my two children, for staying with my grandmother was no longer an option. She would daily say to me that I had to move out and make my own way. One of the statements that I make today is, "Rejoice that trials and tribulations come," because they can propel you to the next level. It appears sometimes that "all hell is breaking loose," but God in His infinite wisdom has a plan.

I was twenty years old, had not finished college, and had no essential job skill sets other than playing the piano and typing. I knew I was an effective communicator and that I was armed with positivity, enthusiasm, and energy to be a success (whatever that took). So, I sought the want ads, and visited offices of business establishments seeking a job.

28

One day on my trek, I stopped in a cleaners owned by a good friend of my aunt and grandmother. I shared with him that I was living temporarily with my grandmother and was looking for a job to move into an apartment and to support my children, as I was not receiving any support from their dad. He said he had heard that Metropolitan Life Insurance Company in San Francisco was hiring. I frankly told him that I did not have any money, much less fare to take the train to San Francisco. He went to his cash register and gave me $1.00 (which was the fare to and from San Francisco on the train). However, it was not enough to take the bus from the train station to the location of Metropolitan, but I thanked him for his generosity.

I accepted the $1.00 with joy, but knew that I had yet another struggle, and that was to get clothes to wear on an interview to San Francisco that was known as the city of best-dressed women. My only solution was to ask my grandmother to let me have the rent money that I paid her ($15.00 a week) that resulted from my work on Sundays as a pianist and choir director for a church in Oakland to buy an outfit to wear. After much persuasion on my part, my grandmother relented and I went to the local Good Will store at the time that had very upscale clothing and goods. I picked out a nice brown suit, hat to match with a beautiful brooch, matching shoes, and gloves that (back in the day) went for a small price of about $20.00.

The next day, I was on my way to Metropolitan Life Insurance Company. I said a small prayer and took the train to San Francisco, dressed in my Goodwill outfit and ready to "rock and roll." The train stopped at Union Station, and as I did not have the bus fare to travel up to Stockton Street, the location of the company, I literally had to walk eight blocks uphill in those high heel shoes to Metropolitan Life. I entered the Personnel Office, whereupon the Personnel Manager greeted me. I shared that I was looking for a job and I had heard they were hiring. She quickly escorted me to her office, remarking she had seen me before and asked if I lived in the San Bruno area (which was an upscale community at the time), to which I responded, "possibly." She stated, "Well you certainly look familiar." We were just about to advertise for someone and we have an opening here in Personnel and if you are a good typist, you can have a job here reporting to me.

My heart sang and I was rejoicing inside. I took an aptitude and typing test and passed them both with high scores. Because of the dexterity in my fingers as a pianist, I passed the typing test with only three errors. I was then asked to go upstairs for a medical exam (which in those days was a requirement for employment). I passed this exam also with flying colors and was told when I reported back to Personnel that I was hired. I knew that God had shown favor on me with the Personnel Manager.

I literally raced downhill those eight blocks in high heels back to Union Station to take the train back to Berkeley. Yes, I had a job as a clerk typist, and I needed to report for my new job in two weeks, and the pay was $450 a month. I was so thankful and excited.

Rejoicing all the way on the train to Berkeley, I was given a jolt when I realized I had yet another hurdle to overcome. I now had to find a sitter for my children because my grandmother had told me if I found a job, she would not care for my children. She stated she was tired and too old to take care of two small children. I clearly understood my grandmother's position and I knew in my heart that God again was on my side and since He had made a way for me to find a job, He would certainly find a way for me to obtain adequate childcare for my little ones.

The next day, I suddenly had an idea to call the Child Care Headquarters in Berkeley to ask for help. I called the office, talked to the receptionist, and made an appointment to see the Director. Her office responded and asked me to come in on Wednesday of that week at two o'clock p.m. What inspired me to have the courage to call the Head of the Child Care Center was my belief that you always go to the head, and I needed help in a big way. I was sure that only God was directing my path.

On that Wednesday I dressed my children in brother and sister outfits (and they looked like twins), as they were only nineteen months apart. I entreated them to be polite and well behaved while we were visiting this lady's office. I arrived early for the appointment, and after a few minutes was ushered into the office of the Head of the Child Care Center. There was a small table and chairs where she suggested that my children sit and play while we chatted. They went quietly and began to play with small toys on the table. I was thrilled that they were so well behaved and obedient.

I quickly shared the story of my husband's abandonment with no child support or visitations, and how I lived with my grandmother, but wanted to make my own way, get an apartment, and raise my children. I shared the good news that I had found a job with Metropolitan Life Insurance Company in San Francisco, but I had no one to care for my children as my grandmother had emphatically stated she would not care for them. I informed the Director that I had heard about childcare centers and came to the headquarters for her help.

I could see she was impressed at my initiative. She listened carefully to my story, asked a few questions about my background, and the area that I lived in. She then picked up the telephone and called a Child Care Center two blocks from where I lived and I heard her tell the person on the phone that she was sending a young woman with two children to the Center. She then asked me to take my children to that

Childcare center on the day I was to report to work at 6 am, and, she also had made arrangements for me to pay (at a discount) for the services when I received my first payroll check. I thanked her, and cried and shouted all the way home with the children looking at me with total consternation.

Yes, miracles do happen, and I sought help with what I thought was my biggest challenge and answers came. A month later, I was blessed to find an apartment with my first paycheck a few blocks from the childcare center. My children were taken care of in that childcare center until the day they both went to public school.

Principle Learned: *You have not because YOU ASK NOT! I asked and I received. Praises to God for his Blessings. Miracles do happen for them that seek and ask.*

Scriptural Reference: *Matthew: 7:7: "Ask and it will be given to you; seek and you will find, knock and it will be opened to you."*

Chapter 7
Knowing that God is a
God of Abundance

Metropolitan Life Insurance Company had hired me with a nice salary at the time of $450.00 a month. I had two small children in childcare near my grandmother's house where I was living. However, I had a dilemma, my grandmother wanted me to move out immediately. I had found the answer, a brand-new apartment complex around the corner from my grandmother's home in Berkeley. The only catch was that I needed a deposit and the first and last month's rent to move in.

At the time I was a church musician and choir director for one of the largest churches in Oakland, receiving $15.00 a week for serving in this position. So, I decided to go to the Board of Trustees and Deacons to ask for a small loan. After making a special appointment on a Wednesday evening, I went to make my request known to the Board of Trustees. I was terrified and was certain they would not want to loan that kind of money to me. All I had to offer was to pay them back in small weekly installments.

However, I gained enough courage to dress in the same suit that I had interviewed for the job in San Francisco, and go to the meeting. I was asked to remain outside until they called me in. About 15 minutes later, I nervously went into the meeting, seated before me were five men. I told my story and asked them to loan me the money, stating that I knew the church was a benevolent entity and I wanted to come to them first.

I looked in all of their eyes and I told them that I knew that I was not an unattractive woman, and I could have gained this money through some other means, but I was NOT that kind of woman and never would be. They looked at me in shock that I had said this and asked me to step outside. I was scared that what I had said was too direct. Not only was I certain that they would not lend me any money, but now I feared I might also lose my job with the church.

In about 15 more minutes, the Chair of the Trustees Board came out with an envelope filled with a check and cash. Inside was more than I had asked for. The Trustees had discussed my faithfulness as the church pianist and choir director, and they all agreed that they wanted me to have enough money to provide for all that I needed. This included food and staples to stock my new apartment. Because my need was greater than the loan, the Chair offered me a part-time job as a clerical assistant to take care of his books, as he was an owner of a large janitorial service. God came to my rescue again with a double blessing.

Principle Learned: Seeking help from the church; letting go of pride, taking control of my life and trusting God led me to experience first-hand that God is a God of more than enough & Abundance.

Scriptural Reference: 2 Corinthians 9:8 "And God is able to make all grace [every favor and earthly blessing] come in abundance to you, so that you may always [under all circumstances, regardless of the need.] having all that you need, you will abound in every good work."

Chapter 8
Understanding and Heeding Your Inner Voice

Understanding self is important, and listening to your inner voice is equally important. Had I heeded this inner voice (really the voice of God) I would have avoided eleven, almost twelve years of pain and suffering. I had every intention of making my second marriage work. I had married an educated man who was very successful, articulate and probably one of the most brilliant men I have ever met. He was well versed in poetry, history, politics, spiritual matters and philosophy. However, he was emotionally abusive; this began to happen during the honeymoon phase.

He became very controlling, monitored my phone calls, and would be abrupt with my former friends. When we first met, he liked the fact that I was a model. As time passed, he managed to talk me right out of my modeling career. So I gave it up, in hopes of appeasing him. At the time I was playing and directing choirs at a very large church. He started being mean about my going to church and would not attend with me. I noticed that for weeks he would be wonderful and nice to me, and then out of the blue, he would become very demanding and angry.

I knew I had not heeded to the voice of God, although at the time I was not aware He was speaking to me. Understand that God is always speaking to us. After many years of painful and emotional abusive experiences in this marriage, I knew that I had to find some way out. We lived a very stable existence in a upper-middle class area and my children were very well cared for. The bills were always paid on time; I used my checkbook like a coin-purse, and would keep writing checks until he told me to stop. He would buy me expensive gifts and cars of my choice and would be very loving at times.

We entertained lavishly. We owned a boat and enjoyed boating and fishing with the children. I even had my own fishing rod leather case with my monogrammed initials on it. We were a bowling family and each of us had our own bowling balls. After eleven years, I began to realize that I had "sold" my soul to the company store.

He was relentless in his controlling behavior and

It grew worse when he took on a very high demanding job. He began to drink heavily and say threatening remarks to me. Even the children began to avoid him and stay in their rooms, studying, and being quiet. I realized that my children were suffering. He had held me hostage for years saying that if I left him, my children and I would have to live in an undesirable area of the town and suffer. He knew that I could not afford to live the lifestyle we were currently living.

I stayed with him because I thought, at the time, that I was giving my children a better life. My daughter was set to go to Spellman College after graduation, and my husband and I were going off to Hawaii for a vacation. My son was poised for Howard University when he graduated and we were able to pay the college tuition. So, I acquiesced and thought I could go through the day-to-day living with him for the sake of my children.

In my pain and misery, with illnesses that ranged from migraine headaches to stomach disorders. One night finally, in utter despair, I cried out to God and prayed asking Him to help me. Although I did not know Him at the time, He knew me. Later, I heard an inner voice saying, "I knew you before you were formed in your mother's womb; I watched you in secret." This was long before I found out this was scripture in the book of Jeremiah, because at the time I did not read the Bible.

I was comforted that night when He answered my prayer. In my sprit he told me to do two things, one, get my teeth fixed, and two, wait on Him. I was amazed. Now, I know this sounds strange, but, I needed to get my teeth fixed. I found out through visiting the dentist during a regular checkup, that I needed to lose all of my front teeth because of a gum disease. I marveled at this, and have later shared in many speaking engagements, that God knows everything about us, even the tiniest minute things. He created us and is concerned about every aspect of our lives - our hearts – our souls - our spirits and even our teeth. He always answers prayers.

I must admit, it was quite a shock and very frightening to think that at the age of 34, I would need upper dentures. However, I was obedient and started the dental procedure that took about eight months. During this time, the emotional abuse increased and I knew that it was only a matter of time. I was waiting and waiting to see what would God do. It was difficult, but I realized in my heart that I simply had to have faith and wait on Him. Finally one night a few months later, we had a terrible argument. I was so frightened, that I left home with my three children and checked into a nearby motel. My two older children seemed scared and very concerned. I consoled them, and shared that things would be okay, and we would get back to normal fairly soon.

When I returned home the next day, my husband said he would leave and let me stay in the house. I was shocked and thought that this was very interesting. He always threatened that if I left him, he would take everything, including the house, all the furniture, and the cars. I could not afford the lifestyle he had given me, and would be forced to live in an undesirable community. Little did he know I was no longer fearful of his threats. I had decided in my heart, that living in an undesirable neighborhood would be better than the "hell" I was now living in. In light of the circumstances, I was completely at peace and could not understand why.

I had one last challenge on the day he finally decided to leave the home. It was extremely nerve-wracking. He had made rude remarks all during the week to get me upset that he was leaving. I made arrangements earlier in the week for the teenagers to stay the weekend with their friends. I also asked my caregiver to keep my five-year-old for the weekend. I did not want them to see any unpleasantness prior to his leaving. He was slowly packing his things and dragging his feet, and he kept saying to me, "Do you realize that I am leaving?" He was drinking and began to yell this all over the house in an effort to get me to respond. So I left the house because I could see that something bad was brewing. He had never struck me, but I felt in my spirit that he would do something violent if I stayed in the home.

I went to my neighbor's two-story home in back of my home, and explained my situation. From her upstairs bedroom window that looked down into my living room, I could see my husband pacing back and forth. I knew that she worked for the most famous civil and litigation attorney in town, so I ask her to start proceedings for my divorce on Monday morning. It was then Saturday afternoon. As she was a paralegal and working on her law degree, she said she would draft up the papers and have them ready for her boss' review by that Monday.

I could see from her upstairs window that he was departing, and I was giving thanks to the Lord that nothing serious had happened. I thought I could return to the house, but when I returned, he approached me yelling again, "I am leaving, do you understand that?" I remained calm, docile, and tried to look loving and contrite as I could. I knew that by being calm that day, and keeping my mind on God's promise to me that I should wait on Him and he would work things out. My husband then finally walked out of the home. I was completely at peace. I could care less about the house. I knew God worked it out in my favor as he was departing without violence and I received the blessing of peace I knew within my heart that there was a better future in store for me.

On Monday, the divorce papers were filed. It was a miracle that the divorce preceded without incidence. Miracle of all miracles, my neighbor's employer, the most famous attorney in the city, took my case without pay, with the stipulation that I would go back to school. During our conversation regarding the divorce, I shared my hopes, dreams and background, and how I had gone to college early and had dropped out and never finished.

During our conversation, he shared with me that he had gone to law school with six children, and a wife at the age of 42. He advised me not to be concerned with my age and get back in school as soon as possible. Further, that I was not to ever sublimate my desires for success to another man. This stunned me as I had known this prominent attorney for many years, but had not realized that he had returned to school in later years and was so successful. I promised him that I would return to college and complete what I had started years before.

Another miracle occurred during this time. God softened my ex-husband's heart during the final divorce proceedings. To the shock of his lawyer, my ex-husband gave me the house, the cars, spousal support and alimony to take care of me and my three children. He stated to me later that he wanted to leave me in the lifestyle the children and me had grown accustomed to. However, I knew that only God was my Helper in this case.

What I learned from this experience is that you must seek help and get direction from God, and be true to your heart. You also must be willing to give up whatever "material" things you may be holding on and you must be willing to *give up* in order to *go up*. I had been holding onto this security for years, taking the abuse, and believing that I was doing it for my children. In reality, when I faced my true self, I had stayed because I enjoyed the financial security and its benefits.

In retrospect, another learning, was when in my heart, I truly made the decision to give up the house, the cars, the beautiful furniture, and the lifestyle I was living. I stayed on point to get on with my life as a single mother and that is when God met me at my point of need. In essence, I did not have to give up; I simply had to surrender to Him and let Him direct my life. Then, I was ready and willing to heed the inner voice, and enter and experience God's plan for my life --- not mine! I knew an incredible journey awaited me and I was excited about the next chapter.

Principle Learned: *You must be sensitive to God's voice, as He will warn you of things to come. If you sense a check in your sprit, do not proceed. I proceeded and ran aground.*

Scriptural References: *Psalm 81:11-13 "But My people would not heed My voice, And Israel would….*

Psalm 32:8-10 "I will instruct you and teach you in the way you should go; I will guide you with My eye."

Proverbs 8:33 "Hear instruction and be wise, and do not disdain it."

Chapter 9
A New Journey
Traveling Within

I was working at the University of California at Berkeley in Electrical Engineering as an Assistant, and with the realization that I was single, alone with two children looking to me for their emotional, spiritual and financial support, I felt overwhelmed and that I must somehow look within. Each night I would put my children to bed early, and then before bed, I would brush my hair nightly in front of a dresser with a very large mirror. One night as I was brushing my hair, I looked in the mirror and I began to ask myself some very pertinent questions out loud, "Who are you?" "Where are you going?" "What are you doing with your life?" "What must you do?" "Why do you feel so incomplete?"

45

I looked in the mirror every night for five days, and then as I stared at the reflection each night, it began to appear as if it was someone else in the mirror. I really scrutinized her, and then I became bold enough to talk aloud to the image in the mirror. I acknowledged the facial features. I studied my nose, my eyes, my ears, my lips, my hair, and I realized one evening that I did not look so bad. It was a somewhat weird experience.

I got bolder. I started more dialogue. I began to ask the image, "What do I really desire?" "What do I like about me?" "What am I really good at?" "What am I doing right now that really feels right for me?" "What do I want to have that's different than it is now?" "Why did I allow myself to become pregnant?" "Was it my choice?" "Can I create the life I now want?" "What's next for me?" "Do I want another marriage relationship?" "Will I be a good mother to my children?" "I never had a teenager's life." "I was still a child myself" What career do I really want?" I then decided to go on a desperate search to learn more about myself, and where to go with my life. I started seeking, searching, and reading every self-help book I could get my hands on, realizing that something inside me was missing and empty.

I somewhat knew from my previous relationships that I had been looking for love in all the wrong places. In earlier years, I had heard in Sunday school the phrase from the Bible, *"Love your neighbor as yourself,"* but I now know that we have placed the emphasis on the "neighbor". The statement is an equation. *If you cannot love yourself first, there is no premise for loving your neighbor.* How different our lives are when we really know and love ourselves and understand clearly what is deeply important to us. Moreover, keeping that picture in mind each day until we manage to do and to do what really matters most, and that is to *Love Yourself.*

As I began to really look on the surface of my life as it was then, I began to feel really grateful not to have someone else's life. In actuality, I had begun a "soul" search. I did not know what I had discovered, but I felt it was a "gift" to me. I had begun to express all of my fears and my mistakes to the image in the mirror. Gradually it became fun as I become more comfortable, and I made faces in the mirror, made jokes and began to laugh at the image of myself.

Out of this inner journey, I emerged more confident. I felt more joyful; I felt alive. I had an expectation each day. I believe people that I worked with noticed a difference, but could not quite put their finger on it. I began to wear more vivid scarfs and colors. I felt victorious – although I did not know how to share this with anyone much less explain it to myself at the time. So, I kept silent about this experience for years. I am sharing this in writing for the first time with the reader. Out of this self-encounter and self-analysis,

I developed a framework to chronicle this experience but kept it locked in my heart.

All I knew was that in desperation at age 23, I had to find that person within that wanted more out of life. I needed to rediscover that confident, energetic, positive young girl I once was. Where was she? Where was she going? What was her purpose? I had wanted my life to count. I wanted to make a difference in the lives of others. Yet, I had ended up getting pregnant at 17, and now at 23, I have two children, I am a single parent, a working mother, and what's next for me?

I did not want to blame my parents, my step-dad, my grandmother, my aunt, or my ex-husband who had deserted me. No, I had to face myself and see what the real challenge was. After the soul-searching experience in the mirror, I knew that I had to take full responsibility for my life and my choices.

A few years later, I discovered from my psychologist colleague that I had unlocked the keys to the power of self-discovery. I had obtained this in a unique way that many of his patients took years to acquire. They needed lots of inward work on the "couch" to process and sort out their lives.

I understand that all of us have biological and neurological origins, with 50% of our personality that is genetically inherited. However, there are other aspects of our personality that are based upon our experiences. If one has a negative experience it can be changed.

What I learned from this experience in the mirror is that basically I was born with the personality traits of an extrovert. However, due to earlier experiences in my life that were dark, I had become pessimistic and thought "dark" thoughts. I soon discovered that I had the "power of choice" to change those dark thoughts, and choose to make better choices for my life. I was in control of my destiny and no one could do it but me.

This was a "heady" experience that changed my attitude and approach to life. I began to consciously use my power for myself instead of against myself. I realized that I could be anything I wanted to be; it was simply my choice. I could become a victim or victor, it was all my choice. It was remarkable that at 23 I began to walk taller and have a sense of confidence in my attitude and talk.

Quite by accident, (but I believe it was yet another miracle in my life) I discovered Norman Vincent Peale's book, *"The Power of Positive Thinking."* I was inspired to take the 30 day mental fast shared in his book. This was an eye-opening experience for me. I had no idea my thoughts were so negative. I wore dark clothing and liked a dark house with the shades drawn. I constantly thought of negative things happening to my small children, although we were living in a safe environment. I was fearful for them to play outside when I was not there.

When I completed the 30 day fast, my thoughts were more positive; I had begun to catch my negative thoughts and reaffirm them with speaking positive words. I started to self-talk affirmatively; I stopped comparing myself with others. I began to use my newfound power to become gloriously authentically myself.

In retrospect, I think about my exercise in the mirror those nine nights or so. To me, it was a miracle that I had traveled that road of looking inward, and uncovering what was real and true for me. Most of all, I began to see that I was already as powerful as I would ever be. I looked in the mirror one day and saw the "real" me. I smiled and smiled! I began to say out loud, "I am more than enough" and I am on this journey to be successful as a human being.

Principle Learned: We are all searching for God. We want to know the purpose of our lives and what leads to true fulfillment. We desire to love and be loved. My journey within led to true acceptance of my self and set me in motion to allow God in my life.

Scriptural Reference: Deuteronomy: 4:29 "But from there you will seek the LORD your God, and you will find Him if you search for Him with all your heart and all your soul."

Chapter 10
It's My Choice: The Fight

After a few years of schooling in a private school, it finally folded and I had to go to public school. I was only six years old and in the third grade. The District school policies dictated that that time that I was too young for third grade and placed me in kindergarten. The kindergarten class was located on the perimeter of the school grounds in a small building. I immediately found out where the third grade class was being held in the main school building; and went there each morning to sit on the front row of the class. Strong willed, I would still leave the kindergarten class and show up every morning in the third grade classroom. I did this for two weeks and would sit on the front row.

The teacher finally so perplexed and frustrated, asked the principal to call my mother to the school. My mother took me to school to visit the principal's office and she was not pleased. She stated to the principal, Mr. Jennings, (I will always remember his name), that I was strong-willed. She explained that I had attended a private school and had completed 2nd grade school work, therefore I should be in the third grade. I knew I belonged in the third grade, and I started to speak up and tell the principal that fact, but my mother gave me a stern look. Mr. Jennings politely stated to my mother after much discussion back and forth, that I would have to undergo a battery of tests to actually ascertain if I could indeed do third grade work.

They scheduled the tests the next week. I took all the tests even though I knew I belonged in the third grade; I had to stand my ground. I knew that I was smart; I had worked hard as a student in my earlier grades, and when the test results were revealed, he was amazed. I was allowed to stay in the third grade. Later on I graduated high school with honors with the classmates I met in third grade at age 15.

Born in the decade before World War II, I came of age during the social, political, and cultural tumult that occurred in America. The number one issue of the day when I was growing up was rebuilding after World War II, and later the fight for Civil Rights Legislation. The Civil Rights Legislation Bill was passed in 1954, which was the year I graduated from high school. I had attended segregated schools all of my early school years and my experiences were positive.

My teachers were all African American, had graduated from Harvard, Yale, Columbia and other eastern universities. They all came back to this small town to give back to the students in the community they once lived.

They instilled in us discipline, academic rigor, and a 'work' ethic of excellence. I graduated with a class of 83 souls, all of whom went off to college. We were nurtured, prodded, and knew from elementary school that we were "college bound." There were no 'if's, and's or but's. We had a rigorous curriculum. I took French, Latin, all the required math courses, and our English and Literature classes were incredible. Our teachers and parents ingrained in us that we were to attend college. Me and my fellow classmates all knew from our teachers that *it was not about going to college, it was about where you were going and to finish college.*

At the time, the status of women in my era was not highly profiled, much less for an African American female. I was raised in the traditional ways of the 1950s. We were programmed to follow a lock-step sequence from college to marriage to motherhood. Like my mother and grandmother, I was expected to go to college, find a husband, and devote my adult life in a career as a nurse or teacher and be devoted to husband, family and home.

Much of what was done or said in the 1950s was governed by inhibition and prohibition, particularly for all females. We were expected to live lives designed by our mothers, fathers, teachers, ministers and peers.

After graduation from high school, I would often remember the fight I had to enter the third grade and how confident and bold I had become and now I was about to enter an unknown world by attending college at age 15. I received several scholarships to major universities, mainly in the mid-west and south and I was accepted at UC Berkeley. At the end of the day, I wanted to get as far away from home as I could. Attending UC Berkeley was also a dream of my aunt who at the time, was attending graduate school there. Hence, she strongly encouraged my mother to allow me to come to Berkeley.

Principle Learned: *That one has to fight for what you want and you must know who you are, what you can do, and where you belong.*

Scriptural Reference: *"Jeremiah 1:5: Before I formed you in the womb, I knew you and before you were born, I consecrated you; I have appointed you to be a prophet to the nations."*

Chapter 11
My Journey into the Occult!

I had gone through several interesting phases and challenges in my life, but I had emerged victorious— although I did not know how to explain it at the time. God's miraculous power brought me through many experiences. He had come to my aid when I needed to divorce my second husband. However, I was not aware that I needed a relationship with Him. I had been in church, served as a choir director and musician for many years, but I did not know God personally.

Going through two divorces had left me feeling emptiness in my soul and spirit. My youngest daughter was a special needs child, having been diagnosed with juvenile diabetes at the age of 8. It was a troublesome and frustrating time in my life. I was then working full-time, going to school full time at nights, and taking care of my daughter.

I had very little help with her care. Many of my friends were afraid to care for her in my absence as she had to be injected with two insulin shots a day. I was lonely and wanted companionship. I started reading all sorts of self-help books and still could not find the peace I was seeking.

I thought I could get answers and gain insights to some of my unresolved issues that were waking me up early in the morning. I began a journey not knowing what I was getting into. I thought that I could help others and I knew I had a gift of what I called, "strong insights" into people, but could not understand how I could meet individuals, feel their pain, and just know what was going on with them. I had on some occasions shocked some of my students with this unwarranted intrusion of information into their lives, and consequently had shut down with this activity.

I sought answers, but in all the wrong places. One of my friends told me about a spiritualist she had visited. This spiritualist was able to state incredible information about her that she could not have known. This lady shared truths of her past and foretold her future. I was intrigued, and went to the person she recommended to get my own answers.

As simple as that, and quite innocently, I got involved with astrology, and spiritualists who claimed they were true believers in God. Thinking this was the solution and the way to find answers to fulfill my emptiness, I accepted them. I also heard about individuals who could read cards and tell you your future. I was intriqued with Astrology and started studying it. I was fascinated by it and began to meet individuals on campus who read tarot cards and some of their friends who claimed they were also spiritualists, "walking in the light," who became friendly with me.

In the meantime, a group of my girl friends and me had all gotten divorced around the same time. We all lived in upper middle-class neighborhoods, and we would get together when we could, drink our wine, and talk about our woes. We would chat about the dynamics of astrology and spiritualism. I talked to my girl friends about the benefits of astrology and how tarot card readers could tell you your future, when you were going to get married, what job or career opportunity that might be coming your way and other answers they might be seeking. Many of them began to visit spiritualists and astrologers believing they were getting answers that were true. Of course, the picture painted for them was always rosy. I would also talk with people I would ask about their astrological signs and provide a mini interpretation for them. At the time, I really believed that astrology was the solution for so many people who were looking for answers.

I found that I somehow knew intimate secrets about students and individuals I would come in contact with. I knew things about them, yet I could not explain how. When I shared with a few of them what I knew, they were shocked. I genuinely believed I was helping people.

One Friday afternoon, I was invited by one of my newfound friends who worked on campus and claimed she was a psychic. We had only seen each other on a few occasions on the campus. She invited me to her home that evening after work. She was hosting a spiritual weekend encounter with a group of spiritualists, psychics, astrologers and various individuals who were walking in the "light" from all over the Northern California area. I accepted her invitation and after work I drove to her home.

When I arrived, there were people doing astral-travel, psychic and tarot card readings, and other things that I have never seen or experienced. My eyes were opened that evening in full force to the reality that there was a supernatural world. My host called out to me and stated there was a woman upstairs who wanted to give me a reading. I went somewhat hesitantly up the stairs to a room where she was seated facing the open door at a table.

However, when she saw me, she started waving her hands, and saying, "Whew, there is too much light around you, I cannot — I cannot... read you and I literally ran down those stairs from that house. I was frightened to my very core at what I had seen that evening. I had never heard of astral travel, and my experience with this lady shook me, but somehow, I felt relieved that she was not able to "read" me.

I began to read all the books and information I could find on the occult and its practices. I discovered, it was defined as "beyond the range of normal perception, secret, mysterious, esoteric, dealing with magic, alchemy, and astrology." I realized that these were the things that I had embraced. Moreover, I realized that I was in error. I was horrified that it was a real journey. I was walking on the "dark" side and was totally unaware of it. Later on, I literally had to denounce all the works and my involvement with the occult. I realized that I had embarked on a search to help demystify human behavior and why individuals behave the way they do. My intentions were to help individuals find answers and peace. Yet, I was easily deceived and unknowingly opened the door to just the opposite.

Since I had proactively convinced a number of my girlfriends to seek astrologers and spiritualists to find their answers, certain they would be helped. I had to go to each of them, ask their forgiveness and share that I was in error and that entering into this realm was nothing to not take seriously. I admonished them that this was a dangerous road to travel. I strongly stressed that they should not involve themselves further. A few of them took my advice; and that was the end of my adventure into the occult.

Because of that experience, over the years, I have been able to share and counsel individuals about the dangers, that many of them have unknowingly become involved with the occult, using Ouija boards in childhood, and in other occultism practices. I always inform them that they must "denounce all of these works." This is mandatory. For you cannot play on the devil's playground and not be affected by it. You must denounce his work and declare his work null and void, and declare the power-working-saving works of Jesus Christ.

Even now in retrospect, I can see how God's hand and His Angels were watching over me and guiding me through this journey. We can go down so many different paths seeking to find answers which only our Creator can give. I do caution people who go down this road to be very careful, because like me, I had no idea what I was going into and the road I was traveling. Yes, indeed for I was on a searching mission that culminated in an astonishing night that ended my short-lived journey into the occult.

Principle Learned: What might seem right in the natural is not in the supernatural. Once you become spiritually alert, the enemy cannot enter your life, so do not open doors that you might not be able to close. The Bible says that God's people will perish for having lack of knowledge – and many Christians are dragging demonic spirits home with them due to their lack of knowledge about how dangerous it is to engage in any type of occult activity.

Scriptural References: Leviticus 19:31 "Give no regard to mediums and familiar spirits; do not seek after them, to be defiled by them: I am the Lord Your God." Ephesians: 4:27 "Neither give place to the enemy"

Chapter 12
The Close Encounter of
the Personal Kind

I will never forget the date, September 6, 1977. I had a personal encounter with God. It was Labor Day weekend and my daughter was away visiting her dad. I went to bed quite early. I was sleeping in my large home alone, when out of the blue I woke up so frightened. This was a rare phenomenon for me as I rarely experienced fear. I had never slept with even a night light on. I tossed and turned and could not get back to sleep. I recalled that the next day I had plans to go shopping for my daughter before she returned. I looked at the clock and it was only one o'clock am.

I laid in bed for a while in the dark, and I began to feel more frightened. When I turned on the light, it appeared that it did not dispel the fear. I became so fearful that I began to sweat. My nightgown became soaking wet. I was now trembling and shaking. I felt an ominous presence in the room and as I opened my eyes, I saw this dark shadowy figure and it appeared to get closer and closer to the foot of my bed. By then I was terrified. Suddenly, I heard a voice say to me, "Get up and go into the living room, and get the tract that was left under your couch in the living room."

Earlier in the week, a very close friend of mine visited me to talk about her new experiences with God. She stood in my foyer with a small pamphlet in her hand and asked me to take it and read it. I had a few choice words to say to her, but she kept insisting that I read this small pamphlet. I told her I would like to invite her in but I had a male friend visiting at the time. She said "Well, I will leave it under your sofa in the living room in case you want to read it later." I had forgotten all about it and had never taken time to read it.

By now, I was too terrified to go into the darkened living room. Then I heard this voice again, so I hurriedly got out of bed. I literally ran down the hallway into the living room to retrieve the pamphlet under the sofa pillows. While reading this tract, I knew that I needed salvation. At that moment, I accepted Christ into my life.

Then, I heard this voice tell me to find my Bible and get in bed. I could not locate my Bible, as the only one I had was on display in the living room and it was massive. I was told to get in bed and lay down. I folded my hands on my forehead and realized that we were having a conversation. (I later knew without a doubt that I was in the presence of God). I became aware that a thought as a question does not answer itself. I admit I asked many questions; "What about my friends?" "What about my daughter?" "What about my love life?" "What if, what if?"

I kept fighting saying "If I go your way, I will have to give up my life style." He answered me saying, "You will not be giving up; you will be gaining." He kept repeating this over and over. I kept asking questions and I was totally honest with Him. He answered all my questions. His voice was so loving and I could physically feel my entire body being engulfed with such extreme love. I surrendered and said audibly, "Alright, you win."

Before I fell into a deep sleep, I looked at the clock and it was 5 o'clock in the morning, yet I had awakened at 1 am in the morning, which meant this encounter had lasted for approximately three hours and it seemed like only five minutes.

When I awoke the next morning at 9 am, I felt completely refreshed and full of energy. I felt like one hundred pounds had been lifted from me. I felt light and free. The entire racing engines in my body had ceased... to just absolute peace.

I literally floated through the house that entire day in complete peace. I knew that a powerful force of extreme love had been poured into me. It was one of the most exhilarating nights of my entire life. I will never forget what I have called," A close encounter of the personal kind."

This was the beginning of a beautiful relationship with Him. I spent time with Him in what I call "spiritual training" for a year. I began having early morning conversations with Him and writing a journal as He suggested. I learned His ways, How his kingdom works, the power of love, grace, faith, and obedience. Moreover, the nature and personality of God, and how to always daily seek His guidance. I was eager to learn and an astute student. He asked me to be open to His teachings and to always keep my motives pure and my heart open to His Love to serve and love people.

My encounter with Him was on a dark night in September some thirty-nine years ago, yet it remains alive and real in my mind as if it happened yesterday. After about a year, He spoke to me one day and said, "I am so real, most people miss me." I chuckled because in one of our conversations, I had told Him that earlier in my life, "I did not think he was really real."

Principle Learned: *God is truly Real And Alive & well. He wants people to get to know Him. It was about a personal relationship with him – not religion as I had known it.*

Scriptural Reference: *Matthew 6:33 "Seek ye first the kingdom of God and his righteous, and all the things will be added unto you."*

Chapter 13

The Beginning of God's Plan

For years, I had wanted to go back to school and finish my degree. I had pleaded with my ex-husband about going back to school. He was always discouraging and wondering why I wanted to go back to college. He would say, "You weren't in college when we met, so why do you want to go to college now?" He was adamant that I not return to college. So for years, I kept silent about my feelings about completing a degree.

I felt like I was an "incomplete" and I had felt this for years. I knew in my heart that I suffered from what I later learned that Dennis Waitley calls "Leaky self-esteem." I remembered that I was smart in grade school and at age six, my mother had fought a battle through persistence for me to attend public school in the

3rd grade. In high school, I had always been outspoken and stood up for my rights and those of others. I knew I had a voice to be heard. I knew deep within my spirit and my soul that there was something destined for me. I knew that there was greatness in me, and that I had to meet my destiny.

My day of reckoning came at age 36 after my personal encounter with God. I heard God in my thoughts, clearly say His plan was for me to go back to college, and complete what I had started at age 15. However, I was afraid, realizing I had to confront my fears because no one knew I had not finished college. I was working as an executive assistant to a college president. Many of the people on campus knew that I had attended UC Berkeley. However, they had never asked me if I had completed a degree, they just assumed that I had. I had not shared this information but, I felt that if people did not ask, I would not tell.

So, with much courage, I went to the see the Director of Admissions who had been my friend and quasi-mentor. I had to share that I had not finished my degree with someone, and I knew he would not judge me nor be shocked. He listened as I wept bitterly in his office. I told him if I went back to college and started taking classes as an undergraduate, "What would people think?" He chided me and said, "Why do you care what people think? Just go and do it." I took his advice and ordered my transcripts.

A few weeks later, he called me into his office. He sat me down, and stated, "I have some good news and I have some bad news. You are admitted, but you only have completed 26 units that are transferrable." I just sat there in shock and finally I asked, "How many units will I need to take to get a BA degree?" He stated, "Well it depends on what major you take." I replied, "I want to get a degree in psychology, and possibly social psychology."

He gave me the number of total units that I would be required to take to graduate with the major I wanted. I was dismayed and very discouraged. I remember, I looked up and it appeared that I had a huge mountain to climb. Suddenly realizing what going back to school would entail, I felt like giving up the goal. I was a single parent, working full-time, raising two teenagers, (one in college) and a young child who was a diabetic. This would mean that I would have to take night classes, and find a sitter for my child at night.

I sat there for a few moments, and left with a resolve in my spirit that with God's help I would and could do it. I began with the end in mind and backed into what I would need to do to complete the degree. I started college in the spring semester with a resolve to get A's in every course. I worked full-time, went to school at night and then after one year, I decided to accelerate the process by taking thirty units in one semester. In order to take thirty units, I would have to submit a petition and appeal to the Dean of the School of Education and have it approved.

Because, I was doing well in all of my courses and currently had a 3.9 GPA, my petition was approved. I was able to enroll in a total of 30 units (five courses), and at the end of the semester, I had completed the thirty units with straight A's. It was an uphill climb, but with God on my side, I knew I could do it. Once we take charge of our lives, and ourselves we can be, do, and have anything we want.

I worked full-time, spent quality time with my children, gave up socializing with friends, studied and stayed focused on my goal of completing the BA. One of my daily practices was to "visualize" myself graduating in my cap and gown and sitting in the stadium with the sun beating down on my face. That is exactly what came to pass on the day of my graduation.

I thought this was an end to the educational journey I had started at age 15. I was then thirty-nine years of age and having a great time with new friends that I had met while going to college. I had been on God's campaign trail for new souls during this time and I was single, free, loving God and my life. Now what? I would have never dreamed of what He had in mind next!

Principle Learned: *Realize that God wants you to be a winner –
but it is not always in the time frame that you have in mind.*

Scriptural Reference: *Jeremiah 29:11 "For I know the plans I have
for you," declares the LORD, "plans to prosper you and not to harm
you, plans to give you hope and a future.*

Chapter 14

My Egypt Experience

I was having a wonderful time as Executive Assistant to a College President while I was in school earning a degree. While I was in pursuit of my Master's degree, I was given a promotion to Job Coordinator in one of the Student Services offices on campus. My assignment was to find jobs as an alternative for students who were not eligible for financial aid. I was in the field five days a week and given a state vehicle to travel throughout the city. I made television and radio appearances on a regular basis to solicit jobs. This job led me to meet with various local corporate officials, educators, and state and government officials. I loved the work and my colleagues. I loved God. He was directing my steps and it was a joyous time in my life.

One day, my world fell apart. Due to the passage of Proposition 13, and severe budget cuts, there were major changes that took place in the university. It impacted a number of individuals, even me. The position that I loved was abolished. My joy had been working with students and community individuals in a very positive and rewarding effort. I was finding job opportunities for students. Now, I was being transferred to an area that I knew nothing about. Thankfully, the department head informs me that I would be trained accordingly.

Furthermore, I was moved from a large spacious office to a cubicle with no windows. I was asked to learn a new task that I actually abhorred. In reality, this became what I called my "Egypt experience." Within two weeks, I knew that this was NOT my calling. I disliked the office, the atmosphere in the office among the staff, and everything about the job. My colleagues were not happy about me being transferred into the office. Moreover I was to be trained by a designated person who had no desire to train me.

The atmosphere was toxic; the students at that time were strident and demanding. The office staff were intolerant. There were snide comments made about the students, many of whom were from low income and disadvantaged families. My immediate supervisor was a female from "hell," or so I thought. I asked God why? He responded, "Do not ask me 'why' questions, ask me 'what' questions." I asked him what to do. He stated, "I want you to love them." You want me to "love them." I shouted, "love people who resent me and are leaving hate notes in my mail box." He kept saying, "love them."

I tried my best to get out of this job. I applied for others and never received an interview. One day, I realized that this was God's assignment for me. I rebelled and was very angry and frustrated for three years. I would go into the bathroom and cry in a stall so no one would see or hear me. I was sorely troubled. God led me to read the allegory, *"Hinds Feet in High Places."* With revelation, I began to understand that "sorrow" and "pain" would be my companions on my journey for years to come.

I finally asked God again the "what" question. He responded and said, "You are to love them. They are being used to shape and mold you for your future purpose." Moreover, He asked me to solidify my love for them with an "act of love." Being obedient, I purchased a small, inexpensive gift for twenty-one people in the office. I carefully wrapped each one, and early one morning before anyone arrived, I placed it on each person's desk. Every gift had a note attached that only said, "You are loved."

This "act of love" freed me to love them unconditionally as God loves us. I truly began to see them in a different light as he has shown me. My entire paradigm was changed. I began to see that they were indeed helping and molding me to step into a greater destiny than I would ever imagine. I learned during this seven-year experience, that you never grow in a "cocoon" or "embryonic" environment where everyone "likes" you. You grow when you are stretched, prodded, and poked to move into action. We all love an environment where we are surrounded by loving people. I was to be a "light" in this office. What I was to do was to learn the lessons that were being taught to me. What were my lessons one might ask? They were lessons in love, patience, tolerance, long-suffering, joy, peace, and forgiveness. It was not easy and I do not mean to imply that it was overnight. The process for me was a total of seven years

I was bombarded with "hate" messages on my desk and in my "mailbox" for being a believer for months. I was set up for failures, overlooked on assignments that I knew I could do, in favor of someone who was less talented, yet, I persevered and stayed the course. A friend and coworker whom I loved and thought was my friend, betrayed me. I was not invited to lunch with any of my co-workers. They were afraid if they befriended me publicly, they would then incur the wrath of the department head. He had so much hostility for me that it spilled over to anyone who was seen with me for any length of time.

There was even during the time that a new employee was hired in the division that I will never forget. She was perplexed and bewildered as she began to notice how I was being treated by all twenty-one members of the department. She came to me and I have never experienced someone who "cried the tears I could not cry" since that time. Again, God moved on my behalf and a book was suggested to me to read. It was "The Spiritual Man," written by Watchman Yee in the early 1900's. It is a slow read and one has to read and re-read to gain the revelation of the chapters. This book gave me an understanding, in depth, of the operation of the spirit, soul, and carnality (flesh) of man.

Oftentimes when I could, I would drive off campus on my lunch hour to a small church that was open, and pray during my noon hour just to get through the day. I never complained to anyone; I only talked to God. It got to the point where my department head and his second in command spewed hatred and disdain towards me during every staff meeting. Since I was not an original member of the FA club, my errors were turned into a spectacle and the staff was my audience.

Yes, the experience lasted for *seven years*. Remember, with every desert experience, there is an oasis. It was after much turmoil and challenge within and relying on God's grace and mercy, that I had to keep humble (being teachable to God), and accept my position as it was. I had to continually give love, compassion and wisdom to the many students in need that came into my office. I also worked diligently to give respect to my colleagues and superiors. My greatest moments were when I began to enjoy my days in this department that I had originally hated. I turned my attention to giving the students the "best" of me, and took great joy in being of service to them each day. It was at this point that I realized that I was "okay" if I stayed in this position and in this department. I was at total peace.

The lessons I had to learn were harsh, nevertheless, I made the choice to be the "best" in a craft I did not like and "excellent." I decorated my cubicle and brought the sunshine in my office through beautiful posters and paintings, thus making every student who walked in my office feel "special" and I offered them the "best" of me. This brought more harassment as many of the students only wanted to be seen by me. However, I was not dismayed by any negativity, and I kept being positive with daily affirmations (which I have shared with many participants in my seminars and workshops).

One of the most powerful lessons I learned during the "Egypt experience" was how to turn a negative situation and a sour attitude into a "positive" one. I self-examined periodically for cancer of the soul and the spirit. I checked myself daily for complaints, contemptuous behavior, criticism, unforgiveness, bitterness, envy and resentment. I made a choice to be "character-driven: rather than "personality-driven." I learned to sharpen my skills in that area, and I learned to be patient, grow and incubate.

Some of my experiences may sound severe, but one has to know that God sees and knows everything.

God's assignment for my training purposes was to LOVE them and concentrate on doing and being a model of "excellence." I had to learn to give up ego needs, pride, recognition, and develop a tough skin to criticism. I was called to be a soldier in His Army and this was my spiritual Officer's Training.

You might wonder did the department head and my associates ever come to accept me? No, they did not, but God always sees and knows what you go through. He is your source and He gives the rewards. He does keep score. The miracle occurred when in my heart, I completely accepted my state of being totally surrendered and found peace. I whispered to God, "if I stay in this department until I retire, it's okay with me."

I had found peace and contentment with my situation. One day, out of the blue, I was offered a position in another department. Initially I refused the offer as it was only a lateral transfer and not a promotion. Later after consultation with my mentor, an Education Administrator on campus, he advised me to accept the offer. He shared with me that, "sometimes you have to move out before you can move up." That was my God answer, and I later accepted the offer. I only asked that God would move me out in six weeks, and that He did.

It was a harsh trial, but the rewards were much greater than I could ever imagine. Four years later, I experienced a meteoric rise and became a statewide higher education administrator. My former department head had to meet with me in many meetings that I chaired statewide. I was never rude or unkind to him. Interestingly enough, many of my former associates retired from that department. I became the only employee who has ever left that particular department on any campus to be promoted to a greater assignment.

Principle Learned: *I was the architect of my destiny. I had to be willing to be excellent in my skills, be my best, make a difference, and choose to serve others. I had to wait patiently for my "season."*

Scriptural Reference: *1 Peter 5:6 "Therefore humble yourselves under the mighty hand of God, that He will exalt you in due time"*

Chapter 15
God's Choice (Not Mine)
A Husband?

In total obedience, at the urging and prompting by God, I ended up going to school for seven years, gaining a BA in social psychology, an MA in Counseling Education. By now, I am doing great on my campus job; my daughter is doing well in school, at age seven, she was diagnosed as a juvenile diabetic, and I had to learn how to attend to a "special" needs child. I had managed to help her maintain an even sugar level with her diabetes, and we are living in a beautiful home.

I am content with my life. I love my job at the university; I have a few good Christian friends, and one special friend, Molly, whom I met in graduate school. She and her husband were devoted Christians, and we had become great friends and lived in the same neighborhood.

Because they knew I was a single parent, they always invited my daughter and me to their lovely home gatherings. I felt very special because I was single, independent, and loving it.

On many occasions, I accompanied them to their apostolic church convocations and conferences. They became like a big brother and sister to me. We shared many wonderful occasions in their home. They became helpers to me when I needed care for my daughter. At the time, I was a church musician and choir director for a local Interdenominational church where Molly's husband, Jim was a great friend of the pastor and served as the Assistant Pastor. Molly and Jim served as my caregivers for Danielle on the nights I had choir rehearsals. Jim also was an appointee of the Governor in the justice system, and he and his wife, Molly are always entertaining folks in their home.

One evening, I stopped by to drop my daughter at their home on my way to choir rehearsal. Molly invited me to attend a political event being hosted by her sister in her home for a neighbor who was a congressional candidate. However, she was in a panic because her sister had invited people (not in their circle of friends) to her home advertising it as a wine reception following the event. Both Molly and had never drank alcohol, much less served it in their home. I suggested that it would be okay and was certain it would work out okay.

After choir rehearsal, I was late arriving at their home. The only vacant seat was across the living room. Molly motioned me to cross the room to sit in that seat. So, I had to walk across the room in front of all the guests to be seated. There was a gentleman sitting across the room from me, arguing with the candidate. He was giving him a bad time. I was a bit taken aback by his jabs and comments to the gentleman while making his speech. He was sneezing and blowing his nose frequently. I took note and thought this man was quite rude.

At the end of the event, Molly's sister leads the gentleman who has been very loud and outspoken to where I was seated. She introduces him by his last name and leaves him standing in front of me looking very distraught and uncomfortable. I was polite and asked him to sit down because he looked so miserable. This woman had just walked off and left him standing in front of me.

At the time, since I did not consider him as my type, I did not have a clue that I was meeting my future husband. During our conversation that evening, I discovered that his wife had died a year or two earlier with cancer, and that had suffered for seven years. I shared with him about God's love, and consoled him. He began to cry. He shared that they had been married for 27 years. I could see that he was obviously still grieving. He later asked to call me sometime just to chat.

Thinking nothing of it, I gave him my phone number. He called about two weeks later, and we chatted on the phone very briefly.

Over the month, we chatted on the phone several times. In my mind, I was helping to counsel a good man who was still grieving over the loss of his wife. When he asked me to go to dinner with him some weeks later, I agreed, thinking I would love to eat a steak. Interestingly enough, I had not eaten any beef or pork meat at that time for three years, and now, I had a taste for a good steak.

When I saw him again, I was shocked, because I could not remember what he looked like. I thought again, he definitely was "not my type." I knew I should let him know that, so he would not entertain ideas about starting a relationship between us. Over dinner, I stated to him that he was a nice man, but I was not interested in any relationship with him or anyone at the time.

How we got together after that night was a miracle of God. He would call me from time to time, and I would counsel him. Unfortunately, things around my house began to break down and would need repairing. He would always call just as something drastic would have happened. I would mention it; he would say he was able to repair it. That is how he came into my life—the repairman. I began to call him "Mr. Fix -it."

Eventually, I led him to accept Christ as his personal savior.

I had no idea he would be my husband until he told me some months later that, "I was his wife" and we would do something about it in the fall of the year. I was stunned, but in my spirit, his words went through me and I knew he spoke the truth! Later that night, I had a little talk with God about this man who had come into my life, and sought validation five times asking for signs if this was truly my husband. Each time I received concrete signs that he was my husband.

I argued and argued with God that he was NOT my type, to which God answered, "You do not know your type." I replied, "Couldn't you have sent me a minister or a popular evangelist as a husband?" "Instead you sent me an usher." God told me, "You look at the outward appearance of man, but I look at the heart." He truly knew my husband's heart and after a strong "talking" and much validation from the Lord, we had a non-dating courtship whereby we talked around my kitchen table about all of our values, dreams, finances, and even child-rearing practices as I had a ten year-old daughter.

Interesting enough, my young daughter encouraged me to marry him, and who had liked him from the beginning, and my oldest daughter wrote me a letter after meeting him one time sharing that this was the only man she could see me with as a husband.

This was yet another validation that this man was God-sent. Douglas and I married after a seven-month courtship around my kitchen table in a beautiful church wedding with my two lovely daughters as bridesmaids. God planned the date, the time, the color of my wedding dress, how my invitations should look, the groomsmen's color of their tuxedos and every detail of my wedding that took place on November 18, 1978.

We had a wedding with both our ministers officiating on a Military Base where my new husband worked and with 300 guests in attendance. It was truly one of the happiest days in my life. I give God all the honor and glory for a loving, respectful, stress-free, and happy thirty-seven-year relationship with a man who loved God and me. It was truly the wisest decision I have ever made and to be obedient to God's choice for me. While married to God's choice for me, God's plan in my life was again being orchestrated.

Although, I thought I was too busy with school, Douglas and I were married while I was completing my Master's degree. I finished it, had a big celebration, and after a three-year hiatus, God led me to pursue a doctorate at USC. When I stated to my husband that we did not have the money for me to attend USC, my dear darling Douglas turned to me and said, "Yes, you are going to USC, that's a fact."

God created a financial miracle and made a way, and I attended USC and completed my work in three years, writing my dissertation in eight months, thanks to Douglas. In fact, I honored him with an "Honorary Spousal Doctorate" at my Graduation Reception. He was with me every step of my journey. He was the "wind" beneath my sails, and I so appreciated him and his enduring love. Douglas and I had almost thirty-eight years of married bliss before he passed on October 13, 2015.

If any women reading this vignette are not married, my advice is to wait on God. You are women on "divine delay." God sees you and know your every need. He will bring you the best and one that is well suited for you.

Principle Learned: _God sent me a husband although it was not my wish to marry again, but more importantly, to accept his choice for me. God ordained marriage to be a metaphor for our relationship with Him (Ephesians 5:31-32). You can be sure that He forms great marriages._

Scriptural References: _Psalm 27:14 "Wait on the Lord; be of good cheer and he will strengthen your heart" Philippians 1:6 "God created someone specific for you and since He is the Creator of both of you we do good with fully trusting Him in this area. He who began a good work will be faithful to complete it."_

Chapter 16
My Tribute to Danielle:
Tragedy of Loss

How can a mother share the tragedy of losing a child? It is not a possibility any mother ever wants to think about. My heart goes out to all mothers who have lost their children. In 1998, my youngest daughter, Danielle died suddenly from the complications of diabetes. She was just thirty years old. I had long lived with this wonderful, gentle, talented, joyful, and enthusiastic young girl. The loss of her has been one of my greatest challenges along my journey. My heart still aches from the loss. It was on the night of her death that the title of this book, *"Dancing on Broken Legs: The Journey of A D.I.V.A."* was conceived.

Some of the many issues I have coached women about have been those suffering from lack of a healthy self-esteem, distrust in a marriage relationship, frustrations about single life, career aspirations, broken relationships, loving self, the lack of commitment from men and women, and the overall lack of morality and ethics. However, one of the most tragic situations that not many women have experienced, is the loss of a child.

Danielle was my third child, born when I was 31 years old. I had been married to her dad for five years, who had expressed when we first married (I had two children, age six and seven) that he did not want children. And, at the time, I concurred. I was very happy with my two children. So, when I became pregnant with Danielle, my husband very quickly said that he wanted me to have an abortion. I was dismayed and frankly heartbroken.

The thought of aborting my baby was disgusting. Moreover, it was illegal and I was not going to have an illegal one. I talked with my Jewish neighbor about this with a heavy heart, and she stated I might have to go to Mexico to have it done. In my heart I knew that I would not be able to do this. I prayed and kept faith. When I was about two months pregnant, my husband came from work and said to me that he wanted to keep the baby. So, joy was in the household when my two eldest children learned I was pregnant. There were so happy and quickly both said they wanted a sister.

In January when I was nine months pregnant, I decided to drive to a store in an unfamiliar area to pick up a stroller I had received at a baby shower. Unfortunately, I ran a stop sign and was immediately struck by a car going about forty miles per hour. I was thrown out of the driver's seat into the street. I landed in the hospital. A few days later, my beautiful daughter, Danielle was born on January 24 looking as if she had two bruised eyes. Her dad was so thankful that both of us were alive and going okay. All of us were thankful to God that she arrived healthy and was a happy baby.

She was a very alert child. She grew to be very bright, articulate and a very communicative young lady. She started walking and talking at a very early age. I surmised this was because she was around her older siblings. Nevertheless, Danielle was extraordinary and had an interesting spirit. When she was six years old, I was brushing her hair in front of a mirror, when she looked back at me in the mirror and said, "I knew you were going to be my mommy, because I picked you before I was born."

At the time, my mother was visiting us and staying in the other room. She appeared in the doorway shocked, stating, "I heard that." I pondered in my heart, what was about this child? When we would visit my grandmother's home, she would say that she would see angels in the ceiling of my grandmother's bedroom. Danielle was extremely bright, intuitive and was very wise for her young age. She would oftentimes shock me with her insights into situations and people.

At age five, I divorced her father and she was very sad. However she was consoled by the fact that he would come to see her once a week, until he moved to another city when she was 7 years old. After he moved, she still found joy and happiness in that she got to visit him during the summers.

At age eight years old, I came home one day and picked her up from her caregiver who had helped me since she was 8 months old. I noticed that she looked thin and frail. I remarked to the caregiver that she looked very thin, to which she replied, "Oh, she is only growing tall for her age." But I began to recall that she had begun to wet her bed every night and some nights in bed with me.

I went home that night, and suddenly I awakened. I saw a man dressed in a white suit, wearing a white hat with a black band around it. As I blinked, I thought I was dreaming. The figure or apparition, I could not tell which, did not move, but kept "looking" in my dresser mirror. I suddenly felt something wet and warm, realizing, "Oh no," my daughter had wet my bed again. I looked at the clock and it was 6:00 o'clock in the morning. I had to be at work for 8 am. I asked Danielle to go run her bath water to take a bath as I changed the sheets.

Normally, I would assist her. As she was a big girl, she always insisted on taking her own bath.

But, for some reason, I walked into the bathroom to assist her and as she stood up in the tub, I almost fainted. Her ribs were showing and she looked like some of the starving children I had seen featured on TV in Africa. I held myself to stop from going into hysterics. I got her dressed and I knew within that she was ill. I took her to the caregiver and stated I have to get her to the doctor, because something is wrong.

She reiterated to me, "She is just getting taller". I knew in my heart that she was sick. I remarked that I was taking her to emergency. My caregiver realized that I was truly upset. I took Danielle to the emergency room of an HMO, that I had never used. (When I was with her dad, we used another HMO provided by his employer). So, when we finally saw a doctor, he did a perfunctory check up and he said, "I think she is just growing, and she is okay." He further said, "This hospital does not have any previous records on her as a patient, so I can not make a complete diagnosis."

I responded vehemently that I knew that this child was ill, and I wanted her tested in the lab for (words I did not even know came out of my mouth), sickle cell, diabetes, anemia, and I was screaming and demanding that he order blood tests be taken immediately. I was literally yelling at him. He was so angry with me; he wrote a prescription for lab work and threw it across his desk at me. He told me to take her to the lab for tests.

When we arrived at the lab, she had to take tests; her arms were so small they could hardly find a vein to insert the needle. I almost fainted. I learned soon after that Danielle weighed almost 68 pounds. During the previous night, she had lost much of her bodily fluids in my bed. We left the hospital and I took her to the caregiver and explained that they took tests and would let me know the results.

The next morning, I received a frantic call from the same doctor who had seen Danielle, asking me to bring her to the hospital right away. He explained that she was in severe trouble. When I arrived at the hospital, she was immediately admitted. My darling daughter was hospitalized for nine days. The diagnosis was juvenile diabetes. Had I not gotten her to the hospital the next day, she would have died. I was so distraught I felt I could not go on. I was working full-time, divorced, going to school at nights and I felt so alone.

Somehow, I found the strength (not knowing then that it was God who was seeing me through). I was able each day to visit the hospital. Her father flew in the next day. We both visited the hospital for nine days, and learned to administer the shots that she had to take twice a day. The hospital informed us that they would not release Danielle until she had learned to give herself the injections. This was to make her responsible for her own illness, which, in retrospect, was a great thing. Danielle was such a trouper, and took it all in stride and after her release from the hospital; she had learned with ease to administer her own injections.

Returning to school for Danielle became a nightmare. Teasing's by her classmates when they discovered she had diabetes and had to test her urine twice a day at school moved me to take her out of public school. I then placed her in a private school where I was assured she would not be taunted and teased about being a diabetic. She would be allowed to take her insulin shots at school and be monitored by a teacher. The headmaster was terrific. On the first day of class, he taught the class about juvenile diabetes, what it entailed, and how Danielle would have to inject herself with insulin, and how she had to be taken care of.

To my amazement, he reported that the entire class voluntarily agreed to take care of Danielle. Over the years, all of them became her champions and caregivers. She quickly blossomed, made great friends, and graduated from her eight-grade class as the valedictorian.

Danielle was very multi-faceted and talented. She excelled in everything that she did. I often wondered about her short life and questioned if all of her early God-given talents were a sign that she would be on this earth for just a little while. When she was nine, she became a champion bowler; officials wanted her to go on the circuit to which I refused; later she wanted to learn to play the piano, she took lessons, mastered it, and was on to the next thing. She wrote a book, played basketball and excelled. She taught herself to paint using crayons to look like watercolors on a canvas. Some of her works were even sold. She painted large paintings and was an ACT-So winner for the NAACP and showed and sold some of her paintings nationally.

In spite of her diabetes, Danielle lived her life to the fullest. She was a joy to be around, always cheerful and making friends. She was a loving child and adult. She was very respectful of adults. She always looked out for me. She called me every day and sometimes twice a day.

Danielle met the love of her life at her first job after college. After a two, almost three year courtship, he properly asked her stepfather, and me for her hand in marriage. We arranged a beautiful wedding for her, and shortly thereafter her new husband purchased a beautiful home for them. A year later, because they had a back house on their property, Danielle and her husband invited her dad to come and live with them. This was due largely to her concern for her Dad living alone with no one to care for him on the East Coast.

What can I say about this young girl, who at age 28 had a brain aneurysm, survived it, with her left side paralyzed, and unable to walk, whose husband learned how to administer therapy for her in the care home and diligently did this every day until she was able to walk with a cane, then steadily, and then alone. However, Danielle never regained the full use of her left arm. She did not let this stop her and she did drive again using her right arm. In fact, she drove 120 miles round trip to see her husband's aunt, whom she loved two weeks before she died. She was a young woman of courage and tenacity.

The most important thing about my daughter is that she knew and loved God. She accepted him at the age of nine. She also loved God, her mom, husband, Ondrey, her sister and brother, her dad and stepdad equally. Danielle loved people in general. No one was a stranger to Danielle. She was an avid reader, and moved with grace and style. She always walked and looked like a model. I was always so proud of her and her graciousness to others.

In retrospect, it seems this wonderful young woman was destined to go to heaven at an early age. We all truly miss her. She will always be in our hearts! What people should know about juvenile diabetics is that rarely do they live past thirty years of age. Many of Danielle's friends that she knew who suffered with juvenile diabetes are gone to be with the Lord!

I know I will see this wonderful child again that I brought into this world. I know that she is up there in heaven cheering me on...

Principle Learned: *God is a comforter, a helper, and one who soothes in times of grief or fear.*

Scriptural References: *Psalm 27:3 "Behold children are a gift of the Lord. The fruit of the womb is a reward." Psalm 91: 2 "I will say to the Lord, my refuge an my fortress. My God in whom I trust."*

Chapter 17
A Mountain Top Experience that Became A Valley

It was in the year, 1977, I was eagerly finishing my B.A. degree and thinking about getting a Masters degree. I was now divorced from my second husband, and I was making progress to meet and step into my destiny. Further, I had a great job at the University and all I wanted was to complete the BA degree.

One night after I came home from work, I put Danielle to bed and went to sleep early that night. I was awakened early in the morning with thoughts about developing these ideas that were coming in my head. Each night for about a week, I would awaken early with these same thoughts going through my head. I could not make any sense out of the thoughts and tried to forget about them.

About two or three weeks later, I was in my office at the university. These same thoughts came into my head and I was compelled to write them down. I quickly took a phone note pad on my desk, as it was the only thing I could write upon, and I started writing, and it was if I was taking dictation. When I came to my senses, I had written on five pages of telephone pad paper – on the front sides and on the backsides. I was startled and I quickly called my best friend who worked for the State Department of Education as a consultant. When I explained to her what I had written, she asked me to type it out and call her back.

I called her back and shared what I had typed, to which she responded, "You have written a piece of curriculum and the evaluation methodology for it as well." I attempted to explain to her what was happening, but was interrupted with a phone call. I was aghast, as I had never written curriculum before in my entire life.

However, the plot thickens, and out of that night experience, I had an idea that came to mind. Armed with new insights about what could be done with the curriculum I had written, I arranged for a meeting with the Dean of the School of Education to talk about a proposal I had in mind that would involve the School of Education.

The day of the meeting arrived, and as I was walking to the meeting site, I actually thought I was going crazy, and that I had nothing to say. My mind was, however, in complete peace. I arrived at the meeting site, and the Dean had called two Department Chairs to sit in on the meeting. I sat down, and in actuality, I really thought I would be thrown out of the office, as I had nothing to say. The Dean explained that I had talked to him about a proposal I had in mind. He had called these   Department Heads to this meeting since he thought they should be involved with a part of the proposal I had shared in my communication with him.

To my amazement, I crossed my legs, and words began to flow out of my mouth with a suggested proposal that involved the School of Education. I explained the proposal in depth and shared that it would   involve   graduate   students   from   their departments. They all were excited and suggested since there were no resources for such a program, that I seek a grant to fund it. We all agreed to call the Foundation office to ascertain if there was such a grant being offered to meet this programmatic need. The Dean picked up the phone during the meeting, and called the Foundation Office. He then handed the phone to me. I inquired if there was a grant that would address what we had in mind. The Director of the Foundation stated yes that there was a grant that we could apply for but it would be due by March 15! That date was three weeks away.

After a brief discussion, the two Department Heads stated they would be traveling to conferences and would not be available to write a grant by the time it would be due. They then suggested that I begin to write it in the interest of saving time. However, they would help wherever possible and agreed to be the two designated academic heads to be implementers of the effort along with the Dean as Director of the Project. The Dean stated he was leaving for Chicago, but would be back in town before the March 15 deadline. In the meantime, he asked again, could I begin to write the grant and he would proof it and make any necessary additions or edits when he returned? I had never written a grant before in my life and I did not even know where to begin, so I answered yes.

I left the meeting in shock. First, I could not believe what had just happened and second; I knew it was not me speaking in that meeting. Words just flew out of my mouth. I was still shaken. I called the Foundation office again that day to get the particulars of the grant proposal, which they forwarded to me. I went home that night, and took out a pad and stared at it. I wondered what to do, and where to start? I remember, I took my pen and a lined tablet, and started to write, and when I came to myself (truthfully) I had written 25 pages, of which I could not remember writing.

This was just the beginning of an incredible journey. When the Dean returned, I had the first draft of the Grant Proposal written. He readily approved it and admired my work (which I was shocked). I was then told all the steps that a grant proposal has to go through, and again I thought I was losing my mind. I had to get signed letters of endorsements from both Assembly and Senate legislators, the Lt. Governor of the State, the Mayor of the city, and the Chancellor and Board of Trustees of the California State University. All of this had to be in two weeks. I did not know who or what was guiding me, but I was driven to continue. Again one early morning, I was guided to draft letters for signatures of the legislators and go directly to the Capitol, to the Senator's and Assemblyman's offices and the Lt. Governor's office.

I drove as directed and to my amazement, there was a parking space directly in front of the capitol (which in mid-morning) is always impossible. I had dressed very severely and carried a black briefcase. I entered the capitol building. Immediately, as almost planned, I ran into several Legislators in the hallway. I briefly and succinctly explained my purpose. I visited both Assemblymen and Senator's offices, as well as the Lt. Governor's Office. Before I left the Capitol, I had signed letters from all the Senate and Assembly members, as well as the Lt. Governor. I was again in shock.

I returned to my car and surprisingly enough, there was no ticket on the car yet the meter had run out. I felt a strong impression to drive immediately to a restaurant nearby and close to the capitol of a friend I knew who was the owner. To my surprise, on a normal

100

busy street close to the capital, there was a parking space in front of the restaurant. By then, I was truly overwhelmed, but excited.

I parked, went in and saw the owner sitting with a customer having a conversation. She hailed me over to join them and asked me, what are you doing downtown during the lunch hour? I immediately got excited and started sharing the purpose and intent for my visits with the legislators and also the Lt. Governor. I then told her that I needed an endorsement letter from the Mayor also, to which she responded, meet the Mayor's wife, she and I was just having lunch and a chat. I almost fell off my chair, and the Mayor's wife said to me, if you want to get in touch with my husband, here is his telephone number. This is his private line and I am certain he will be interested in helping you.

Well I left that restaurant in a whirl and my mind racing. I wanted to shout to the world what an experience I was having. When I reached the university with signed letters, I made a call to the Mayor, to which he responded, "that his wife had shared with him about me and what I was doing, and he said, "Send me a draft of the letter, and I will have a courier get my signed endorsement back to you as soon as possible." Now I knew I had one last hurdle, which was the CSU Board of Trustees. How could I get to all of them? Well, years earlier, when I was an executive assistant to the college president, I had met many of the younger staff members who accompanied the Chancellor to the campus. Over the years, I had kept a connection with one of the staff in particular who had become a good friend.

I made a quick call to my friend's office, got him on the phone and explained my mission, what was happening, and what I needed from the Board of Trustees. Wonders will never cease, he stated the Board of Trustees was meeting the next day, and he would present my proposal before the Board to get their endorsement. The next day, I heard from my friend that the Board had approved and given its endorsement of the proposal since it involved the use of graduate students and faculty to assist in a community-based effort.

Now, I had all the required materials to complete the grant proposal and get it ready to send to Washington. We actually made the deadline of March 15. I understood that if approved, the project would begin effective July 1. Moreover, normally grant proposals, if not funded, would come back in mid-June.

However, something happened later in March. One of the Senators that I had visited and shared the proposal to get his signature, called me and suggested he would propose a Senate Bill if I would take the program I had shared to his district constituents in Los Angeles. I readily agreed and I was in total amazement.

He followed through and advanced a Senate Bill with a budget request of $125,000. This called for me to appear before the Assembly Rules Committee and the Senate Finance Committees to lobby the bill! So, I went to the capitol to lobby the bill, and many thought I was a Lobbyist. Yet, how could I explain this to anyone and make sense of what I was doing?

In short, I made presentations to both the Assembly and Senate and the Senate Finance Committees. The bill passed both houses. The bill was sent the Governor's desk for approval. However, at the same time, Proposition 13 – (The Gann Initiative) was on the ballot that year and it was passed affirmatively. Consequently, my bill was not approved due to the passing of this Proposition.

I was still hopeful of some positive outcome for the Grant Proposal that was submitted to Washington DC. Word had not come back approved or denied, and it was now June 30. The Dean explained to me that more than likely the grant was approved in that it had not come prior to June 30. However, the grant proposal came back on <u>July 3</u> denied.

For some time, I would revisit these occurrences many times over and over in my mind. I could not imagine what was happening. I wanted to share about what had occurred with me, however, every time I would attempt to share, I would hear these words, "Do not caste your pearls before swine." I felt like I was operating with an "energy field" surrounding me. People actually could not get within three feet of me. They would recoil as they felt this energy. I was told by many of my colleagues later that during that period, it was as though I was encased in an energy field.

So, although at the time I was not walking with God and did not know Him, but I knew one thing, that it was not me, and that all of these incidents were the miracle workings of God. He was using me as a vessel to get a message out and a program to help individuals who were in need of such services, using university graduate students as the implementers to do great work in the community. Why did he choose me? I cannot even answer that to this day. Most certainly, He was the orchestrator and designer of all the work that was done and I was only His vessel.

After this experience, I understood clearly beyond a shadow of doubt how great works that were done by ordinary individuals were all guided and directed by the sprit of God. He and He alone moved on them to write beautiful music, poetry, paint the Cistern Chapel, make beautiful sculptures, and create inventions to help mankind! It was all God who created man and imbued him with various gifts of purpose. If one yields and submits, they can do wondrous works on this earth.

I believe He knew that one-day, I would know Him and do His works but it was not the time. Soon after, I went into "my Egypt experience" that lasted for seven years.

Principle Learned: *Sometimes we lack the wisdom, experience and humility for a call to greatness. The blessing may be delayed, but it will come! One must accept whatever circumstances you find yourself. Stay positive, change your paradigm and know that God has a specific time, plan and design for you to step into and fulfill your destiny for greatness.*

Scriptural Reference: *Jeremiah 29:11 "For I know the plans I have for you," declares the LORD, plans to prosper you and not to harm you, plans to give you hope."*

Chapter 18
Speaking Words that
Landed me in Africa

I had never wanted to go on a cruise nor thought about traveling on one. I had several friends who always talked about their cruises and the fun they had, but I was never intrigued by the conversation. I was not afraid of the water and I had been on several boats, and actually gone deep-sea fishing in the Pacific Ocean where the waters were very rough. However, cruising on a ship did not appeal to me.

However, due to the constant invitations from my close friend, she actually persuaded me into going on my first cruise. It was a networking cruise for professionals and the ship was traveling to the Caribbean and departing from Florida. I was finally going on a cruise and I had just re-careered from my 36 years of serving in education. I asked myself, what am I doing going on a networking cruise? What will be the benefit for me? I am no longer working in a profession. What can I offer?

I shared with one of my best friends my dilemma, and she stated you must have some business cards to take with you on this cruise. Tell them that you are a motivational speaker. I was hesitant because I was currently teaching only two classes at the local university as an adjunct professor. I kept telling her that I was retired, moreover, who wants to put "retired" or "adjunct professor" on a business card? She kept insisting and as I was nearing the departure date, she volunteered to go to Kinko's to get some business cards printed. My friend came back later with cards that read, "Motivational Speaker", with my name in bold letters and a Post Office Box address. I was still reticent, however, between my friend and husband's insistence, I took them with me.

There was a grand reception the night before we departed from Florida. I had a chance to meet and greet many other travelers from across the United States. There were numerous celebrities, authors, attorneys, nurses, congressional leaders, doctors, university professors and others who are all on the cruise ship and successful. I also met a young women traveling alone from Kenya. She and chatted at length that evening and I marveled that she had the courage to travel such a distance to come on this cruise alone without any of her friends.

On the day of the cruise, I did get very excited as we departed the Port in Florida. Once the ship was well underway at sea, we were all called to gather in the main salon. Our hosts greeted us with enthusiasm and excitement. We were told it was now sharing time. All the guests were to go to the podium to introduce themselves. Each of them gave their names, and shared their professions. I was very impressed with those aboard and was thinking, "not one of these folks have even mentioned the word retired." I quickly assessed that that they were not only all working professionals but high profile individuals. There were numerous famous personalities on the cruise.

When I stepped up to the podium, I hesitated on what I should say. I cleared my throat and spoke loudly and clearly, who I was and that I was a motivational speaker from California. My thoughts were that I had spoken to many groups and corporations while working in higher education, but I had never considered or called myself a motivational speaker. I remembered I had business cards as well. I spoke those words and remembered later that in the scriptures, we are told, *"The power of life and death is in the tongue,"* and to *"Call those things as though they were."* Well I called my future with those words being shared in the universe.

The next day, I ran again into the young woman I had met from Kenya. She shared that she had come on the cruise alone and that she was celebrating a major birthday. She wanted to go on a new adventure and meet new friends. She asked for my business card. Every time I would see her on the ship, she was always laughing, and appeared to be having fun. I would smile and take time to chat with her briefly. She was always beautifully dressed and I would compliment her about her beautiful outfit. I noted that she was not seated at the captain's table and that she was not ever with the so-called "in crowd" on the ship. However, we always managed to bump into each other during the course of the cruise. She saw me one day and said, "I heard you speak in the salon when we were out to sea that you are a motivational speaker. Would you come to Kenya and speak to mid-level women managers?" I replied, "Of course I would love to come and I know of the president of the country."

She shared that she was a business owner in the city of Nairobi; she had great corporate contacts and knew that many of the women would love to have a person of my caliber come and speak to them. I was thinking that she would just chatting and was probably flattering me.

The cruise went remarkably well with no incidents. I met many new and interesting people. I thoroughly enjoyed my inaugural cruise. When I returned back to the states from this exciting new adventure, I was more than ever impressed with cruising and vowed to go again.

A few months later, I received a call from the woman I met on the cruise from Kenya, asking if I would come to Nairobi to conduct a seminar with female mid-level managers in December. Because I declined stating I was unable to travel in that month, she invited me to come in May of the next year and I agreed. I had no idea of what I was getting into, however, we began conversations back and forth for the next few months. We finally agreed on a mutual date and I departed to conduct a two-day retreat in Kenya. However, it was not with mid-level female managers as I had thought. It was with higher level individuals from Fortune 500 companies and members of the Parliament of Kenya.

The primary lesson I learned on this journey was that my "words" spoken on that ship a year earlier launched the beginning of my international journey as a motivational speaker abroad in many African countries, including Senegal, Tanzania, South Africa, Benin and Abijon.

Principles Learned: *Words you speak have power – when you share positivity about yourself in the universe, it gives you back what you say. And, always be generous and kind to those you meet for you might entertain an angel of help unawares.*

Scriptural References: *Proverbs 18:21 "The tongue can bring death or life; those who love to talk will reap the consequences" Hebrews 13:2 "Be not forgetful to entertain strangers: for thereby some have entertained angels unawares."*

Chapter 19
My Journey to the
Continent of Africa

I believe each and every one of us is born with a life purpose and a dream. Somehow, that dream can become so buried that we never realize it nor pursue it. My dream simply was that I wanted to make a difference in the world.

My dreams, however, never included going to what some would say, the "motherland, - AFRICA. I had been given an opportunity to go to Africa twice during the early stages in my life. I had turned the first offer down with circumstances that prevented me from accepting the second offer. Now, with a third offer, I found myself on a plane with a 27-hour flight to get to my destination. I never had a desire to visit the continent of Africa. I am now flying to conduct a two and half day leadership retreat with mid-level professional women managers in a country I never imagined I would go.

Needless to say, I had an uneventful flight on British Airways; a stop in London to get refreshed, and another eight hours on Kenya Airways. I arrived in the city of Nairobi on a balmy evening. Once through customs, I saw my friend whom I had met on the ship. She and many other people were waiting at the airport to welcome me to Kenya. It was an exciting time and I found the weather was very much like California. We traveled to my lodgings where she was my host and they were very comfortable and I felt very much at home.

The next day, I was given one of the Kenyan newspapers and a magazine. I saw my pictures in the newspaper and a layout of me (centerfold) in Kenya's True Love magazine, that was similar to the Essence Magazine in the United States. I was amazed. I found out later that evening as we watched television that I was on one of the Kenya TV channels with commercials about my visit to Kenya.

I was stunned as the picture they used of me was an old one that had me with "big" hair. It was the only one I had sent them that could be used at the time. I could not believe it. However this was indeed a very humbling experience! I was billed as "American Motivational Speaker comes to Kenya." However, there was still a surprise in store for me.

On my third day after some rest, I was taken to the conference site located on the outskirts of Nairobi. It was a magnificent Resort, which was so amazingly beautiful that I was speechless. It had a golf course, lake and the entry and rooms were all beautifully decorated. I checked out the conference room that had been reserved for the retreat. It was enormous with lots of lighting that I liked. I asked if there was a CD player for music, as I normally used music in all of my retreats and seminars for mainly women in the states.

My seminars were always done with my "theme song." I would always enter the room dancing and I would encourage all of the seminar participants to dance for about 5 minutes. I had learned that this exercise connects the triune brain in people to get them excited and enthusiastic! It was what I called my "undercover" praise and worship sessions since many of my participants were from different faiths and backgrounds.

I looked across the room and there was a young African gentleman working with the CD player and sorting through CD's. There was some music playing softly. Much to my amazement, my theme song by BB and CeCe Winans that I used in the states was being played. I knew then without a doubt that God was in the mix. This was my confirmation of His involvement. I was destined to be in this country, in this place, and I was overwhelmed and thankful.

Given the tradition in Kenya, my host and I had agreed to begin the weekend event on Friday with "high tea." So, I was very excited and knew that with the music, this would be a good introduction for the opening of the retreat on Saturday morning. I would be well prepared to come in dancing to my theme song. I was feeling very pleased that all seemed to be in order.

I was not prepared for what I saw on that Friday afternoon as I waited in anticipation of the arrival of the guests. I saw several Mercedes Benz cars entering the circular driveway with flags flying on them. I surmised that this fabulous Resort was possibly hosting dignitaries for a Friday afternoon meeting or a weekend event. I stepped out of the room to check the registration tables in an adjourning room. There were lavish leather briefcases, and an assortment of gifts and pins. All my workbooks and materials were prominently displayed for the participants. Everything appeared in order. Staff from my host's company was dressed professionally, and ready to check in the guests for high tea, and I was at ease that all was well.

It was then that I noticed that a group of men were entering the lobby coming towards the registration desk. My host came to me and explained that the retreat had included members of parliament and CEO's from various companies in the city who had paid and wanted to participate. There were only a few women CEO's attending and I was stunned.

I immediately fled to the powder room and began to cry. Looking in the mirror, I said to the Lord, "You have got the wrong person." What can I teach these members of Parliament and CEO's from Fortune 500 companies?" I have nothing to say to world leaders. I heard Him clearly say, "It is not about YOU, it is about ME!" I dried my tears, powdered my face, and went back to the room thinking, "Okay, God You are on."

The female Minister of Transportation for Kenya, saw me and said, "If you have attended one of these seminars, you have attended them all." I was really dismayed then. Putting on my full armor, I geared up as I knew that God was in charge and to place my trust in him. It was His show. I began to pray fervently as I saw the room was full.

There were 35 individuals who attended for the two and one-half days. I will not describe all in detail what happened, but I did enter the room on Saturday morning dancing. They were a bit surprised, but as I got them all up dancing, they began to enjoy it. For the entire weekend, during the sessions, we danced. They loved the workshops and they all said there was very informative and new information and insights shared about leadership from a different perspective. They were excited and engaged. As the time passed, one could feel the spirit of God in that room. I knew that God was in control.

Reporters from the Newspapers and Television personnel from various TV stations came on Saturday night to interview the participants and me. I was a nervous as I did not know what responses they might give to the questions being asked by the press. However, later that night on the news, I saw the amazing interviews and comments while I was in a restaurant. All of the participants stated, their lives were changed and it was akin to a spiritual experience. Praises to God. It was amazing to see Him at work.

A point of reference to note is that the Minister of Transportation, who had made an initial comment about the event, said at the conclusion of the retreat that "she truly had learned some new things about herself and her leadership style. Further, she had amazing feedback and insights into her personal style of interacting with people like no other seminar on leadership she had ever attended."

She became my most ardent supporter. She extended invaluable courtesies to me via her staff at the airport when I left Nairobi. For me, the weekend was a blur. I was exhausted, but joyful and happy that the retreat was so well received.

On that Monday night, I was scheduled to speak to a group of women at the Stanley Hotel sponsored by True Love Magazine. What I discovered was many of the women in the audience were the wives of the men that had participated in my weekend retreat. In that it was a city holiday the next day, I talked for about two hours, and the women had more questions and did not want to go home. So, I stayed and answered their questions, as I was received with such great enthusiasm and love. Three or four of the women shared later that their husbands came home "changed," and they were very happy. They asked me, what did I do? I merely told them that I had shared insights about internal leadership with them from a new perspective and that it was God in the mix.

This inaugural trip to Kenya changed my life. As a result of the overwhelming responses from these women who were hungry and seeking more personal and spiritual growth I developed and implemented with the help of my friend, the DIVA's dinners. The next year, I traveled during a set period of time in May or June each year. I conducted them for 13 years. Today I have an alumni group of successful women throughout Kenya who attended these dinners with Dr. B (as I am called).

Over the years, they have all shared how their lives were changed by my ability to share with transparency, authenticity, wisdom, my love for God, and the wisdom and spiritual principles I have learned walking with Him. More importantly, imparting to them that we women in the United States grapple with the same challenges, concerns, dysfunctional relationships with our men and sister friends, family issues, child rearing in today's climate and environment, as well as how to establish a closer relationship with God.

I tell them that our lives as women, in many ways are no different from many of theirs. I have been fortunate in my journeys to Africa these past thirteen years to not allow my self to be limited by traditions and preconceived ideas. Moreover, to be open, love unconditionally, and to let go and let God direct my words to say and my paths to follow.

While traveling a continent I never wanted to visit. I came to love it; enjoy its people, and embrace them as my sisters and brothers. I have experienced events that have propelled me to share my journey. I have met with presidents and leaders of many countries; held workshops and conferences with men and women in leadership positions with government and corporate entities.

In 2014, The US Ambassador of Senegal invited me to kick off the USA Corporations Week in Dar-Salaam, (a 99% Muslim country) and present a message to the Ministers in the Cabinet and CEO's of corporations which I titled, "The Transformational Success Journey." The Cabinet Ministers and the 450 attendees had never heard of an American Motivational Speaker. Yet, they enjoyed it and many stood in line just to get my autograph on a newsletter/handout I shared with them about the Creator. I am pleased to share that my speech is now in the library of the University of Dar-Salaam for students to listen and share its message.

The Ambassador of Abigon in 2015 invited me to speak at a World's Investors Conference. I was one of the panelists to share on this international platform with people from all over the world. Because the language of the country is French, as they do in Senegal, both of my presentations in Senegal and Abigon were partly in English and French with the help of an interpreter.

An interesting footnote to share with you is that a year later, when I traveled to conduct my second Leadership Retreat with leaders, I learned that prior to my first trip to Nairobi, Kenya, the PR and planners of the Leadership Retreat attempted to research information about me and could not find anything about Dr. Young. At the time, I was retired and there was not any information about me listed on the California State University Chancellor's Office website. Further, there was no record of me as a university adjunct professor at California State Dominguez Hills University, in that CSU Universities did not list adjunct professors on their websites. Consequently, the planners and officials asked my host if I was legitimate in that all these dignitaries were coming to a Leadership event with no information about Dr. Young.

My point is for many of you who will read this vignette is to know that God always has a plan and a purpose for you. It is not conventional; his ways are unconventional. I did not have a website; I did not have a Public Relations person nor an Agent. I was not an author with a best-selling book on leadership or life-growth. I had the greatest PR person that ever lived and He was in the planning. I was destined to travel to reach the people He knew would be receptive to me. He had prepared me for the job. For fourteen years, I had taught leadership courses, had conducted seminars for corporations in the United States; I had developed original materials for my seminars and workshops that were God-given and unique.

Did I believe I was able to do it? Did I think I was prepared to stand in front of world leaders and CEO's and give them information on leadership? I certainly did not think so. However, God knew and validated me in that one weekend retreat with the 35 individuals who left the event "changed" with new insights about them personally and professionally. Only the Creator himself could have done that. I was only a vessel that was used to make a difference in the lives of those men and women who were attending that weekend.

In reality, God heard me many years ago, and it was my words that started my journey for destiny comes out of your heart. "I wanted to make a difference in the world by delivering inspiration, hope and empowerment to men and women with results one country at a time." I am still in wonderment and am thankful to God for my incredible experiences in my journeys to the Continent of Africa!

Principle Learned: *Oftentimes, success happens when you give into it and when you make yourself available and open to opportunities. You must be willing to do whatever it takes to pursue it without a promise of success, money, or any expectation whatsoever. My journey to Africa taught me humility, extraordinary faith and the opportunity to change lives in a major way, by sharing my experiences, my faith, and teaching the Word of God using practical and creative ways to impart it.*

Scriptural Reference: *Colossians 3:23-24 "Whatever you do, work at it with all your heart, as working for the Lord, not for human masters, since you know that you will receive an inheritance from the Lord as a reward. It is the Lord Christ you are serving."*

Chapter 20
Stepping into my Destiny

Some amazing occurrences have happened in my life. This is one that I rarely share and that is my meeting with Maya Angelou who became my first mentor. Meeting Maya Angelou back in the late 60's was truly a divine encounter. I heard she was coming to the campus as a Poet In Residence, but I did not know that we would have a chance encounter meeting that would lead to me stepping into my destiny.

At that time, I was Executive Assistant to the President of the College. I was taking a walk to the dining commons and approaching me was Dr. Eugene Redmond, a faculty member in the English Department. Accompanying him was Maya Angelou. She saw me from a bit of a distance, and said, "Who is this beautiful creature coming towards me," to which

I responded, "It takes one to know one." Dr. Redmond introduced us and instantly we connected. She invited me to come to her office and chat with her. She wanted to know all about me, as I was the Executive Assistant to the President and one of the few African American females working at that capacity on the campus. I was impressed with her voice and presence.

I visited her a few weeks later, where I shared my story with her; how I had attended UC Berkeley at fifteen, stopped out, and was now feeling like an "incomplete." I told her I felt I could not go back to finish my degree on the campus, because many people had assumed that I had one to be in role I served as Executive Assistant to the president. I started crying. She shared with me a bit of her life story, and cried with me. She stated emphatically, "You need to go back to school and finish. You never quit, and you are not an incomplete." You must polish your gifts and finish what was started within you and God will help you do the rest." People cannot define who you are if you know who you are. Face the truth and let people think what they will. I left her office in tears, but with a new determination to confront my fears, and go back to college.

This encounter let to her inviting me to many visits to her home. I was surprised when she first asked me to visit her. She lived in Napa Valley and it was a long drive for me, but nevertheless I was excited to visit her home. I met her mother, her son, and her then husband, Paul. At one of her soirees that she was known to give frequently, I met the legendary James Baldwin who was her guest. I was ushered into a room where he was by himself and smoking a cigarette. I was in awe and did not know quite what to say to him. I stuttered and said something to him about reading his book. He was so gracious and kind. He later read from his book to the entire group.

This was an exciting time in my life, and later I introduced Maya to one of my sister friends. Maya was delighted since she was as tall as Maya and me. We both would be invited from time to time to her home. I was happy because I had someone to car pool with. Later, I received an autographed copy of her first book. We lost contact when she left the university and over the years when she later moved from Sacramento to back east.

Some years later, I had moved to Southern California and was in a department store in Beverly Hills, when I heard my name called, and it was Maya. I was so excited, and she was so impressed when I shared that I had not only completed and received my BA degree, but had finished my Master's degree. I saw her a few times later when she came into the area to visit her friend. I truly believe God allowed us to meet again so I could share and tell her how I had accomplished not one goal but two, because she planted the seed of confidence within me to be all that God has called me to be.

Because of the impact, she made on my life with her frank approach and input of encouragement to me, I had started my journey to finish my education. This was a very critical period in my life and one of the decisions and choices I had to make on how I would shape my future. I thank God for the opportunity to have met her. Truly she was a blessing and this was a part of my life that I have rarely shared, as it was so "special" and private to me that I did not have a need to blast to the world that I knew Maya Angelou in her early life, and loved her.

I knew deep within at an early age that I had been given a gift to use to help people, and I had been given a lot of energy and enthusiasm. Somehow, I had been derailed; did not know where to start and how to get back on track. I knew I needed to finish college, but had not shared my feeling of being incomplete with anyone. After my meeting with Ms. Angelou, sharing my heart and not only hearing her advice, but putting action to it, I realized that I, and I alone could choose to be the solution to my future and there was much work to be done.

I firmly believe each and every one of us has been given a precious gift or gifts. We are expected to make full use of any gifts God has given us to help mankind on this earth. Oftentimes, circumstances happen; people and things get in the way of our progress into our purpose, but ultimately the choice is always ours to make.

The choice was mine to make to face up to the truth that I was hiding and I had to give up pride, ego, face myself first, confront my fears and not be concerned about what people would say when they found out that I did not finish college. I made a choice to re-enter college, and I when I completed my degree, I experienced the freedom of choice. To know that the secrets to success lie within, in your choices, your ideas, your imagination, your energy, and your instincts toward exploring, innovating and stepping into your destiny. Eleanor Roosevelt once said, *"One's philosophy is not best expressed in words; it is expressed in the choices one makes."*

In the long run, we shape our lives and ourselves. The process never ends until we die. The choices we make are our ultimate responsibility.

Principle Learned: "People come into your life for a reason and a season, not necessarily a lifetime." We have the freedom of choice. No one makes you do anything. No, you choose. Serving God is a choice. He does not force you to love Him. He does not force you to serve him. My choice was to serve Him and in doing so, step into my destiny!

Scriptural Reference: Psalm 16:5 " The Lord is my inheritance and my cup. You are the one who determines my destiny."

Chapter 21
Walking in my Soul's Code

I am walking in my purpose as an exhorter, an encourager and mender of ruined houses. Translated, this means I am a woman who inspires, motivates, and helps people to restore and transform their lives. This is the assignment God gave to me in 1977. When you engage in work that taps your talent and fuels your passion that rises out of a great need in the world that you feel drawn by conscience to meet, therein lies your voice, your calling. I believe this is your "soul's code". I know there is a deep yearning within each of us to find our voice in life.

Like many individuals, I have had heartbreak and tragedies with the loss of my mother, father, two sisters, two brothers, my daughter, some of my best sister friends, and my loving husband. My mother was one of nine children and all of them are gone to be with the Lord. I have a surviving brother, Major, cousin, Coco and her brother, Art. Many of my nieces and nephews who are doing well. We are a blessed family.

Each day, we make assumptions that we will have years to live this life, but life is a vapor. There is a temporariness of life. I believe that God is expecting more out of our lives than breathing and eating. Life is too short. I hope you readers of this book don't let it pass you by. I posed this question many years ago. How am I going to live my life? Am I going to use the time I have on earth to do something good? Will I pursue worthwhile objectives? What do I want to accomplish before I leave this life? I concluded some time ago that life has to be more than clothes, houses, and possessions. I wanted to live a life giving and serving to others. At age nineteen, I declared I wanted to "make a difference in this world." I did not know how, I did not know when, but I knew this was what I was born to do.

I understood early on that we determine the nature of our lives by our choices. I realized the power of choice in one's life in my mid-30's. I had a powerful encounter with God, the creator, and I was given a choice. Why I fell in love with God was because He gave me the wonderful power of choice. I Chose! I even chose to love Him. He did not force me to love Him and to make a contribution on the side of good.

I have spent over three decades of speaking, teaching, consulting, coaching, and mentoring. Most importantly, experiencing real-life lessons in the trenches with many hardships and struggles. I have shared many of them with you through the vignettes in this book.

My view of success is radically different from most individuals. For me, it was and is the success of being myself and allowing the internal me to grow, to develop in the security of who I am, and to whom I belong. Over the years, in my seminars and work-shops, I have always pointed out that people define "success" in different ways. I firmly believe success should be defined by your own terms.

I chose to be successful, and believed I could make it happen. For me, it meant internal growth and development over the years. It also meant I had to study, work harder than anyone else, put my ego in check, love and accept others who did harm to me, and separate them from their actions and keep loving. I believed that I had what it took – the abilities, inner ego strength, talents and skill sets to accomplish my goals. I determined I would make a difference in the world, reach for the stars, and most importantly, be the best "me" I could be.

I consider myself "successful" today because of "where my thoughts and words have brought me." "I will be tomorrow where my thoughts and words will take me." As it states in Proverbs 18:21, *"The power of life and death is in the tongue and those who love it will eat of its fruit."*

"Everyone chooses one of two roads to life – one is the broad, well-traveled road to mediocrity – the quick fix; the other is the road to greatness and meaning – the process of sequential growth from the inside out."

In retrospect, looking back over my life lessons I share in this book, I had a burning desire in my heart that I wanted to make a difference in the world at the age 19. I wanted to make my life count. I did not know what that meant. After wandering off course for a number of years in my early adulthood, I finally chose to start a new journey in my late 30's to make a difference. Maybe because it was my "age of reckoning" or what I have since called, "the time for my transformation."

I made a choice to follow God, and my transformation story is simple. "I was a caterpillar, crawling, inching along each day, then I went into a seven-year cocoon of caterpillar mess. I had to change my old self-concepts and limiting beliefs. I struggled for three years not realizing that I was being groomed and trained to emerge as a "beautiful" butterfly.

This process allowed me to emerge stronger in my belief that I mattered, that I could accomplish anything I set my mind to. I changed my language from

"I can't" to *"I can do all things through Christ who strengthen me."* I had adopted a new mindset about my workplace environment, my co-workers, and I was totally at peace.

When I looked in the mirror, I saw someone different, stronger, bolder, brighter and lighter in spirit who was fierce, on purpose, and a warrior for God.

The following are principles I have shared in many of my seminars around the world:

- Having to change my vision of self

- Knowing & Loving Self – Old Adage – "To thine own self be true."

- Knowing Who I Was (Accepting me, warts and all) being grounded and rooted in Love!

- Understanding that love, peace, joy, patience, compassion was a part of me!

- Changing my negative thoughts to positive thoughts (30-day mental fast to accomplish this).

- Learning that you are where you are because you want to be there. If you want to be somewhere else, you will change. (Finishing my college degree)

- My understanding of the Importance of Affirmation — making positive statements daily about my goals and myself.

- An affirmation is a statement of belief. Without it, the subconscious is free to be programmed by others as to what to believe. Since the subconscious is untrained, it believes whatever happens to be poured into it. If it hears negative comments, then it begins to think negatively. If it is told that you are withdrawn, unsure, self-conscious, and helpless, it believes that and you act accordingly.

- Negative input from the conscious mind results in negative output from the subconscious mind. It's the old law of cause and effect.

- Cause and effect are one. The challenge is that too many individuals only see the effects. They only see what the subconscious had wrought.

- I began to understand and learn that if things go wrong, we lose. If we fail, we tend to look only at the effect and many never realize that there was a *cause of that effect.*

- The old adage states, "If you change the way you look at things, the things you look at will change." However, I learned *it is how you look at things* that can make the world of difference in how you behave.

- What you speak about when your guard is down is a good gauge of what is in your heart.

- Your mind needs exercise just as your physical body does. To keep your body healthy, you must be careful what you put into it and you must exercise regularly.

- To keep your thoughts pure, you must guard what goes into your mind.

- To exercise your mind, you must contemplate things that are noble, and truths that stretch your mind. If you keep focusing on negative things, you will inevitably be a negative person. I fought this fight with 7 days of positive thinking, catching my thoughts, and not allowing a negative thought to enter my mind. I won!

- The *Mind Keeper* is what I call your most powerful weapon. I had an epiphany about this one morning and wrote an article about it. I wish to share the concept with you who are reading this book.

- Keeping your mind is your responsibility. You take ownership of what goes into it; you must have a mindset for success and keep your mind focused and positive. I know it is challenging at best and it takes work, yet it can be done.

- The Manufacturer's Manual, Philippians 4:8 states that, "whatever things are true; whatever things are noble; whatever things are just, whatever things are pure; whatever things are lovely; whatever things are of good report, if there is any virtue and if there is anything praiseworthy, to meditate (think) on these things."

- Choice is most important. What you fill your mind with is a matter of choice. Choose to concentrate on the magnificent truths of God and they will create in you a noble character that brings glory to God.

- Become the *Mind Keeper* and exercise your most powerful weapon.

In the words of great philosopher, Solotan Olatunbosun, "Watch your thoughts, they become words, watch your words, they become actions, watch your actions, they become habits, watch your habits, they become character, watch your character, it becomes your destiny."

Chapter 22
Words of Wisdom
from Dr. "B"

Empowerment is an overused word today. To empower one is to give them encouragement and hope that they can first transform themselves for more success! They will ask how?

Transformation must occur first, and again they will ask how? The Manufacturer's Manual states, *"Be ye transformed by the renewing of your mind."* Consequently, He, who has made us, has given clear instructions that one must have a mind shift to a new mind-set.

You must manage your input to create an output for a desired positive outcome. You need "positive" input to create a new mindset. How do you get this? By what you read and see, and it requires you doing the work!

Books, Television, Media, lyrics of songs and even other's opinions are the input to the product (YOU) for a desired outcome (i.e., success, confidence, faith, and better performance as a human being). Successful Peak Performers practice their craft. They are passionate, energetic, excellent in their performance, enthusiastic, focused, and know their territory. In other words, they know their assignment on earth. What is yours?

Ask yourself these questions. What are you really good at? What excites you? What are you passionate about? What motivates you? What do people frequently come to you and acknowledge you for? By answering these important questions for yourself, you are on the journey of discovering your purpose. Know that the seed of purpose was planted in you from the day you were born.

The Master Craftsman Himself placed you on this earth lovingly for a purpose. You were not sent here merely to occupy space. For if that is the case then "you are here on earth enjoying an illegitimate existence."

I am excited each day as I face new challenges on my continuing journey with God! I am excited about the future and I trust you are as well. I am pleased to share with you some principles I learned on the transformational success journey and I trust these will be of help to you.

- Seek God first; find your identity in Him.

- Know who you are in Him.

- Know what matters to you.

- Know your destination – the road map should be clear.

- See the images of your future and write them down; make the vision plain.

- Face your past; forgive and release past hurts and people who have hurt you to move into your future!

- Seek the *"process of transformation"* that entails a mind shift and new habits. Habits can be changed.

- Make success a priority and develop a mind-set for success.

- Write a total truth letter to yourself!

- Be candid. Read aloud. Burn or tear up letter and release!

- Acknowledge your challenges and confront them.

- You must believe in yourself and know that the *impossible is possible!*

- Develop your inner and the outer being (spirit, soul, and body).

- Reflect daily on the inner (spirit) and what's inside of you.

- Many individuals do not want to deal with their inner soul (Deal with it!).

- Remember, the outer man expresses what the inner man cannot handle.

- Heed the words you speak in unguarded moments. The power of life and death is in the tongue. Speak life!

- You must be your own best cheerleader and perform daily positive affirmations until you get it in your spirit!

- Write your daily affirmations on a 3x5 card and practice aloud each day.

- Remember, there are no quick fixes in the world.

- If you have a need, ask God in faith.

- God will meet YOU at your Faith and not your NEED.

- Tears do not move God; it is your FAITH that moves Him.

- We are spirit beings having a human experience in an earth suit for a divine purpose.

- Tapping into our spirit is living in the divine purposes of God.

- Walking in the Spirit is living by our intuition not our feelings or our emotions.

- The Spirit must remain in the dominant position and in control.

- Remember to meditate no less than five minutes each morning before arising.

Chapter 23

Sacred Principles Learned

During my early 20's there were some powerful lessons I learned. Our parents programmed many of us. I don't know about you. I was not given a choice by my parents, asked my preferences or granted my requests. I was told to eat whatever was put in front of me, speak when I was spoken to, wear what I was told and my wants and desires were not important. We were programmed at schools as well. In school if the teacher called on you frequently, you were called the "teacher's pet." You were told to do your own work and act responsibly. If you asked your classmates for help, you could be accused of cheating. I learned rather quickly that it was not okay to ask a stupid question in my classes, as the teachers would give me one of those "withering" looks and the other kids would laugh.

We are programmed each day by social media and the major media. Many doctors still, I believe program us. Very early on in my family, we learned that the doctor was God. We were to do what he said. We were told the doctor did not have time for foolish questions. You were just to follow the regime that was given and not to question the prescription.

In today's times, we're programmed by fear with help from much of the media. For some of us, it's fear of failure – If we try and don't succeed, then we fear we might embarrass ourselves. For some, it's the fear of success. Succeeding might be even more fearsome than failing. We all need to conquer our fears — one at a time. Fear of failure or fear of success, the simple truth is that most of us just don't dare to have, do or be what we really want. Nothing out there is holding us back. We are holding ourselves back.

The first time I heard the acronym for the word "fear" (False Evidence Appearing Real) was stated by Joyce Meyer. Fear creates roadblocks, stumbling blocks, and leads individuals to self-defeating behavior, which in turn, produces guilt and anxiety, which can lead to complete immobilization.

Fear keeps individuals from trying, and if they don't try, they never get beyond where they are now. One must come to realize that fear can be overcome and defeated as long as you realize the source of it is inside, and not out there in the world. Franklin Delano

Roosevelt addressed the subject eloquently in one of his fireside chats when we said, *"The only things we have to fear is fear itself."* Napoleon Hill wrote, *"Confront your fears and you can make them disappear."*

In an earlier vignette, you learn that I had to confront my fears about returning to college at an older age; leaving an emotionally abusive husband after many years, and then returning to school at age 51 to obtain a doctorate. I made a choice to not live in fear. I took small steps of faith in the beginning and then bigger steps of faith as I grew spiritually. It took courage, years of patience, perseverance, hard work and sacrifices. I made a choice to take charge of my life, find my voice and 'just do it.' Because of it, I achieved my goals and I am truly walking in my purpose today.

My "sacred" principles that I hold near and dear to my heart are as follows:

First things first

- Having a growing, thriving, personal relationship with Jesus Christ, nurtured daily through bible reading, prayer and meditation. This is vitally important for you if you want to integrate your faith and career successfully.

- Forgiveness is a choice. You must choose to forgive no matter what; the choice is yours to become the "whole" person God purposed you to be.

- Always remember that God created you just as you are and He loves you, no matter what others may think of you. Keeping that in mind, you do not have to please anyone but Him. This is a freedom lesson.

- Be grateful for the good things about your life, your job, your family, your children and your friends. In any situation, it is just as easy to focus on the positives as the negatives. Be positive, be grateful, and practice positivity daily

- Learn from bad times. During a particular difficult time or situation in life, ask God, "What am I to learn from this situation?"

- Treat your life as a "whole." You will not find balance in your life unless you treat it from a holistically frame of reference. We do not live for God from 8 am to 5 pm on Sunday and go to work on Monday. Weave everything in your career, your life style, your family, and your commitment to God. Work them all in your life.

- Learning how and when to say "No." I have never been as efficient as I was when traveling, working, attending school and raising a family. I had to learn what to say "no" to and work is the same way.

- Learn to use your "gifts and talents" for God wherever He puts you. This is one of the biggest challenges I had to learn. God does not care where you work or your profession; what He cares about is that you serve Him wherever you are.

- Trust Him with all your heart and lean not to your own understanding. Remember, he has ordained your steps and his ways are not your ways. Do not try to figure him out!

- Seek His guidance and your goals daily. Strive less and trust God more. I read this once, "if you want to make God laugh, just tell Him YOUR plans."

- Be anxious for nothing – husband, wife, cars, houses, career, fine jewelry, fine clothes, but in everything by prayer and petition, and with thanksgiving, present your requests to God. If you are single and want a husband, and/or a wife, you are on "divine" delay. Wait on God.

- Always remember, you are His chosen vessel and He has a purpose and a plan for your life. Truly you can be the "salt" of the earth. Make a vow to be both "salt" and "light" without leaving a "bad" taste in the world.

Chapter 24
Reflections on the
Career Journey

I had a successful and distinguished career that spanned more than 39 years in higher education. I began working in academia at the University of California, Berkeley. After six years, I relocated to Fresno, California, where I found work at California State University, Fresno. Two years later I relocated to Sacramento where I began work as the Executive Assistant to the President at California State University Sacramento. Over nineteen years, I worked in the following capacities – Executive Assistant to the President, Coordinator of the Student Employment Center; Associate Director, Financial Aid, and Associate Director, School College Relations and Outreach.

In 1986, was appointed as the Statewide Assistant Dean of Academic Affairs for The California State University system. The CSU is the largest senior system of higher education in the country with 23 campuses throughout the State of California. I became the first African American female appointed to that position. In 1990, I was promoted to Associate Dean. In 1997, was promoted to the Director of Community and Alumni Relations.

While serving in these administrative positions, I concurrently served as an Adjunct Professor in the College of Business and Public Policy for California State University, Dominguez Hills in Carson, California. For more than 14 years, I taught undergraduate and graduate courses in Administrative Leadership and Behavior, Psychological Dimensions of Organizational Behavior, and Human Resource Management. I re-careered from the CSU system in 2000 to become an entrepreneur.

During the course of my academic career, I was instrumental in developing and implementing various initiatives as follows:

- In 1983, the innovator and creator of an inaugural outreach program to 8th graders at California State University, Sacramento. This program was implemented in 22 middle schools in the Sacramento Unified School District. This campus wide effort utilized well over 150 faculty and professional staff.

It was the first outreach program to middle schools to involve faculty from a CSU campus. This program received statewide recognition and was replicated on other CSU campuses.

- In 1986, launched a statewide middle school effort and named it the "College Readiness Program" (CRP), which was the first Early Outreach Intervention outreach program to middle schools implemented by the California State University system in partnership with the California State Department of Education.

- The program was later expanded to well over 281 middle schools throughout the state in partnership with 9 CSU campuses. During its initial phase, the program received national attention and was featured on the front page of the *Wall Street Journal* in 1987.

- Developed early outreach materials from the booklet, *FUTURES*, and produced videos in Spanish and English designed for middle school students and their parents. These booklets and videos were widely disseminated to middle schools throughout California.

- Served as Chair of the Statewide Cal-SOAP Advisory Board that worked with under-served students who wished to pursue post-secondary educational opportunities.

- Served as a member of the California Intersegmental Coordinating Council and was instrumental in the naming and development of the "College Making It Happen" program from its inception.

- In 1991, created and founded the Long Beach Chapter of Lambda Kappa Mu Sorority. Concurrently with the founding of this chapter, I created and founded the *Alpha Omicron Middle School Mentoring Program* administered by the Long Beach Chapter.

- Program involved 24 eighth grade African American girls from two middle schools in Long Beach, California. This effort was implemented without funding and through the personal efforts and resources of myself and 12 other African American women professionals. These eighth grade girls were mentored for four years and all entered higher education institutions. The program became the national model for Lambda Kappa Mu Sorority. Similar mentoring programs were launched in its 25 chapters around the country.

- In 1991, elected President of the Association of Pan African Doctoral Students (APADS). Served as President of this organization for four years. This non-profit organization program assists Pan-African and African American students who are pursuing doctorates through a community-based mentoring program.

- Pioneered many educational initiatives that have involved middle school, high school and community college students; counseled numerous college students on preparation for college and served as a mentor.

- Instrumental in motivating numerous K-12 students to pursue higher educational opportunities.

- Served as a keynote speaker on many higher education institutions and facilitated sessions on effective leadership, career preparation and planning. Recognized as a highly effective caring professor and mentor.

- A staunch supporter of higher education with significant contributions that brought recognition to the California State University system.

In February 2003, I founded Young Enterprises to provide specialized life growth/empowerment and leadership seminars for professional women from a "holistic" perspective that included "body, soul and spirit." Young Enterprises became a multi-faceted consulting company that provided many coaching/speaking services locally, nationally, and internationally.

In May 2003, the company expanded its services to the Continent of Africa, providing professional and life/growth development for women along with Leadership Training/Retreats for business and corporate leaders. These services were provided in countries such as Tanzania, Kenya, South Africa, Senegal, and the Ivory Coast.

I also developed a leadership and team building series for business and professional women, corporations, non-profit agencies, community groups, women's organizations, city municipalities and churches nationally and internationally.

In 2004, launched a motivational "expo" for women throughout six California cities. These expo's allowed me to use my leadership and personal/professional life experiences to create and deliver powerful, dynamic, interactive seminars.

In 2005, was appointed by former Chancellor Reed as a Consultant to the CSU African American Initiative.

This initiative was created to raise the awareness of the low enrollment of African American students in the CSU system. As a result, with the help of one of the CSU African American Presidents, the CSU African American Initiative was created. With his help, I developed what became the "signature" component *CSU Super Sunday* that was launched in 2006. Super Sunday is an annual outreach effort to students and families through African American churches.

Four other program components were later created and launched in 2007. This effort has helped to give information to parents and students to prepare themselves academically for college. The CSUAAI has been extremely well received and has brought the CSU national recognition. In 2008, I was invited to Kentucky to share the efforts created in California that resulted in the system adopting and replicating the Super Sunday effort.

My career journey has also included my participation in a number of professional organizations. I have served on numerous boards in various capacities that include some of the following:

- West Angeles COGIC Board of Directors (January 2008 – 2010)

- National Institute for the Advancement of Minority Health and Minority Medicine, Serves as Board Secretary (2003– 2008)

- National Certification Commission of Strengthening & Conditioning (NSCA), Board Member, Served as its Public Member (2003-2008).

- Vice President, Goodwill Board of Directors of Long Beach (1999-2004).

- President of the Board of Directors of LEADERSHIP AMERICA (2000-2002).

- Member, LEADERSHIP AMERICA Board of Directors – (1999 – 2004).

- Public Member, California Respiratory Board (1994-1997) first African American Woman – appointed by Assemblyman Willie Brown).

- Public Member National Respiratory Board (1997-2003) first African American Woman appointed in its 40 year history.

- Member of the Delta Sigma Theta Sorority, Rolling Hills, Palos Verdes Chapter.

- Founding member of the Long Beach Nu Lambda Chapter of Lambda Kappa Mu Sorority.

- Listed since 1977 in WHO'S WHO IN BLACK AMERICA.

- Appeared on numerous TV shows and radio broadcasts in local, national and international countries (1970-current).

- Former *Radio Talk Show Host* of Inner Light Radio and LA Talk Radio.

- President/CEO of Transformation Success TV, and is the producer and host of her own show, THE TOTAL WOMAN on one of her seven channels.

- Syndicated on-line Radio Talk Show host of the show Transformation for Success. Interviews each week dynamic guests from television, movies, arts, theater, entertainment, news media and individuals who have inspiring stories of life transformations.

- President/Founder of Success 4 U Foundation, established in 2011 to reach teen girls and their parents from impoverished communities through its Teen Leadership Academy.

My career trajectory has been on an upward spiral for 20 years, and I spent a total of 43 years in higher education, before re-careering again to embark on a journey as an Entrepreneur, International Life Coach, Speaker, Transformation Success Expert, Author, Radio Talk Show Host and now President/CEO of an on-line TV network and Producer/host of a TV Show on one of its eight channels. I am humbled and grateful know that the journey of transformational success happened in my life after I released the reins of my life to my Creator – God.

Next steps – Media Mogul on the campaign trail as God's Ambassador to create spiritual and transformative change in the lives of individuals worldwide.

Chapter 25
My Final Word

These vignettes are some of the lessons I have learned during my journey for the past 78 years. I have changed my life dramatically by the grace of God. I have accomplished many of my goals, suffered many setbacks only to make comebacks and the most beautiful thing is the love that I have for people. Yet I still have a desire to "make a difference in their lives and the world". I have a long way to go to reach my goals, even at my age and I will probably never be satiated because there is still so much of God's work to do.

Thankfully, I have two fantastic adult children who are my friends, my prayer warriors, who surround me with love, and are my ardent supporters. They even have served as my employees at various times.

They are constantly encouraging me and we enjoy our times together. As a family, we have shared many wonderful experiences over the years. I am still learning, growing, sharing, and caring.

What has resonated with me over the years is knowing myself. I firmly believe that affirming one's self, setting goals, and conquering one's fears are the first principles in setting your vision to accomplish your dreams and to make a difference.

It's so easy today to get caught up with the "activity trip" "social media" and in the busy-ness of life. Many have worked harder and harder at climbing the ladder of success to find out it was leaning against the wrong wall. I learned that it is totally possible to be busy without being effective.

People find themselves today achieving victories that are empty; successes that have come at the expense of things they suddenly realized that were far more valuable to them. People from every walk of life – doctors, academicians' actors, politicians, business professionals, athletes and plumbers – often struggle to achieve more success, higher incomes, more recognition, or a certain degree of professional competence; only to find their drive to achieve their goals blinded them to the things that really mattered most and are now gone.

How different our lives are when we really know what we value and what is deeply important to us.

Keeping that picture in mind, we manage ourselves each day to be and do what really matters most. If the ladder is not leaning against the right wall, every step we take just gets us to the wrong place faster.

If you carefully consider what you want to be said of you in an imagined funeral experience, you will find your definition of success. When you begin with the end in mind, you will gain a different perspective. I have given many seminars and workshops over the years, and have taken the participants through an imagined "funeral" experience. It is interesting how many of them experienced an "ah ha" moment as to what success meant to them, or what it means to live a successful life.

The basic premise of my message in this book is to help you reach your full potential and be successful as a person in any capacity of your life – business or otherwise. My ultimate goal is to inspire men and women to reach for higher levels of success in their lives spiritually, emotionally and physically. Success is the progressive realization of a worthy goal or idea. Unfortunately many people do not ever take the time to develop a worthy goal or idea to strive for. As such, their success is limited to what they observe others having and doing. Success for these individuals is external and not internally defined.

If we find ourselves striving for goals that others have decided are important, we lose our dreams and

158

we lose the ideals that would have made our lives an extraordinary and meaningful experience. A friend shared with me that It has been said, "that success in life is based on the capacity to continuously start over." One has to periodically ask, "What do I need to learn new?" "What is it I need to let go?" "What would be valuable to hold onto?" Letting go is hard to do, and it was one of my life's lessons as my identity was tied up in these behaviors.

Letting go for me was a deep leap of faith. Would I be a successful? Would I be able to take care of my children as a single parent? The questions were non-stop; but I discovered, you must let go-to-go up. Let go of what is not working and learn new ways and behaviors.

Become a self-master, trusting God your Creator, yourself, and your intuition. Be open to new ideas; be determined, disciplined, defining your core values and connecting with them. You must never ever quit or give up. Dare to live your dreams. Learn to listen to the inner voice, and learn to learn.

Too many people view life as an opportunity to manipulate others into doing things to accommodate them. There is so much misunderstanding, that hinges on the difference between love and anti-love. Love is not a gushy word, that describes a world of rose-colored glasses, beautiful flowery bouquets and Shakespearean sonnets. True, "love" is a word that is tossed around lightly today. People all around the globe are looking for love. Everywhere you turn, someone is using that word, I love my new car, I just love chocolate, didn't you just love that movie? I wish I could love my job more.

Love is the most basic component of life. Love can only be love. However, it is an action verb. It must be something that you do, not something that is done to you. LOVE IS GIVING – NOTHING more, certainly nothing less. Love is an action and that action is giving in a   special way.

Filling your own cup first with loving you is a primary success tool that I believe in – wholeheartedly. Unless you learn to love yourself first, you cannot love anyone else. Why?

Imagine yourself as a cup. If you fill your self-cup to overflowing, you cannot keep from spilling all around yourself. If your cup is empty, you cannot share your resources with anyone else. It's that simple. Fill your own cup first. It all starts with you.

If you don't do it for yourself, you will spend your life looking elsewhere for conditional love (anti-love) or you'll be looking for love in all the wrong places. If you do not love yourself, you cannot give out true love to people, no matter how much you desire to.

For years, we have heard the phrase from the Bible, "Love your neighbor as yourself," but we have wrongfully placed the emphasis *on the neighbor*. The statement is an equation. If you cannot love yourself first, there is no premise for loving your neighbor. The cup must overflow everywhere. You must love everyone unconditionally, or you cannot love any one. I had to learn this lesson in many ways.

The more you love yourself and fill your cup first, the more you have to give. Only when you lose yourself can good things happen. You alone are responsible for living your life and for your own happiness and contentment. You cannot live totally for others (which makes you a taker), nor can you use others for your own self-affirmation. You cannot be happy being what you think others want you to be, for what they want usually is not what you are. You must accept and love yourself as you are before you can accept and love others.

My thoughts as I conclude this book is that "life may not be the party we hoped for, but while we are here, we might as well keep on 'Dancing on Broken Legs', and take that journey to become a D.I.V.A."

Principles Learned
&
Scriptural References

Chapter 1
The Journey Begins

Principle Learned: *I felt special growing up and I just knew I had a destiny to fulfill at an early age and dreamed about it.*

Scriptural Reference: *Jeremiah 1:5 "Before I formed you in the womb, I knew you; before you were born, I consecrated you; I have appointed you a prophet to the nations."*

Chapter 2
The Lessons

Principle Learned: *It was my early training and recognition by my family and others of the gifts I had been given.*

Scriptural Reference: *Luke 12:48 "...Much is required from those to whom much is given, for their responsibility is greater"*

Chapter 3
Secrets of the Sacred Family

Principle Learned: *Bad things happen to "good" people. However, for growth to become whole forgiveness is a choice; it was up to me. I had to choose. Resentment and bitterness is poison to the soul, spirit and physical body.*

Scriptural Reference: *Matthew 6:14-15 "For if you forgive other people when they sin against you, your heavenly Father will also forgive you. But if you do not forgive others their sins, your Father will not forgive our sin!"*

Chapter 4
The College Adventure

Principle Learned: *Happiness like unhappiness is a proactive choice. We are free to choose our responses to any situation. The choice is ours. We are really the sum total of the choices we make; the ball is always in our court.*

Scriptural Reference: *Psalm 37:39 "But the salvation of the righteous is of the Lord, he is their strength in the time of trouble."*

Chapter 5
My Struggle comes in Trios

Principle Learned: *That God Intervenes on our behalf with people, even our family members, yet our responsibility is to keep loving them, and to trust and have faith in Him!*

Scriptural Reference: Romans 8:28: "And we know that God causes all things to work together for good to those who love God to those who are the called according to His purpose."

Chapter 6
Miracles do Happen for them that Seek

Principle Learned: You have not because YOU ASK NOT! I asked and I received. Praises to God for his Blessings. Miracles do happen for them that seek and ask.

Scriptural Reference: Matthew: 7:7: "Ask and it will be given to you; seek and you will find, knock and it will be opened to you."

Chapter 7
Knowing that God is a God of Abundance

Principle Learned: Seeking help from the church; letting go of pride, taking control of my life and trusting God led me to experience first-hand that God is a God of more than enough & Abundance.

Scriptural Reference: 2 Corinthians: 9:8 "And God is able to make all grace [every favor and earthly blessing] come in abundance to you, so that you may always [under all circumstances), regardless of. things at all times, having all that you need, you will abound in every good work."

Chapter 8
Understanding and Heeding Your Inner Voice

Principle Learned: You should always be sensitive to God's voice, as He will warn you of things to come.

If you sense a check in your sprit, do not proceed. I proceeded and ran aground.

<u>Scriptural References</u>: *Psalm 81:11-13 "But My people would not heed my voice, And Israel would…. Psalm 32:8-10 "I will instruct you and teach you in the way you should go; I will guide you with my eye." Proverbs 8:33 "Hear instruction and be wise, and do not disdain it."*

Chapter 9
A New Journey – Traveling Within

<u>Principle Learned</u>: *We are all searching for God. We want to know the purpose of our lives and what leads to true fulfillment. We desire to love and be loved. My journey within led to true acceptance of my self and set me in motion to allow God in my life.*

<u>Scriptural Reference</u>: *Deuteronomy 4:29 "But from there you will seek the LORD your God, and you will find Him if you search for Him with all your heart and all your soul."*

Chapter 10
It's My Choice: The Fight

<u>Principle Learned</u>: *That one has to fight for what you want and you must know who you are, what you can do, and where you belong.*

<u>Scriptural Reference</u>: *Jeremiah 1:5 "Before I formed you in the womb, I knew you and before you were born, I consecrated you; I have appointed you to be a prophet to the nations."*

Chapter 11
My Journey into the Occult!

Principle Learned: *What might seem right in the natural is not in the supernatural. Once you become spiritually alert, the enemy cannot enter your life, so do not open doors that you might not be able to close. The Bible says that God's people will perish for having lack of knowledge – and many Christians are dragging demonic spirits home with them due to their lack of knowledge about how dangerous it is to engage in any type of occult activity.*

Scriptural References: *Leviticus 19:31 "Give no regard to mediums and familiar spirits; do not seek after them, to be defiled by them: I am the Lord Your God." Ephesians 4:27 " Neither give place to the enemy"*

Chapter 12
The Close Encounter of the Personal Kind

Principle Learned: *God is truly Real And Alive & well. He wants people to get to know Him. It was about a personal relationship with him – not religion, as I had known it.*

Scriptural Reference: *Matthew 6:33 "Seek ye first the kingdom of God and his righteous, and all the things will be added unto you."*

Chapter 13
The Beginning of God's Plan

Principle Learned: *Realize that God wants you to be a winner – but it is not always in the time frame that you have in mind.*

Scriptural Reference: Jeremiah 29:11 "For I know the plans I have for you," declares the LORD, "plans to prosper you and not to harm you, plans to give you hope and a future.

Chapter 14
My Egypt Experience

Principle Learned: That I was the architect of my destiny. I had to be willing to be excellent in my skills, be my best, make a difference, and choose to serve others. I had to wait patiently for my "season."

Scriptural Reference: 1 Peter 5:6 "Therefore humble yourselves under the mighty hand of God, that He may exalt you in due time"

Chapter 15
God's Choice (Not Mine) A Husband?

Principle Learned: God sent me a husband although it was not my wish to marry again, but more importantly, to accept his choice for me. God ordained marriage to be a metaphor for our relationship with Him (Ephesians 5:31-32). You can be sure that He forms great marriages.

Scriptural References: Psalm 27:14 "Wait on the Lord; be of good cheer and he will strengthen your heart" Philippians 1:6 "God created someone specific for you and since He is the Creator of both of you we do good with fully trusting Him in this area. He who began a good work will be faithful to complete it."

Chapter 16
A Tribute to Danielle: Tragedy of Loss

Principle Learned: *God is a comforter, a helper, and one who soothes in times of grief or fear.*

Scriptural References: *Psalm 27:3 "Behold children are a gift of the Lord. The fruit of the womb is a reward. Psalm 91:2 "I will say to the Lord, my refuge an my fortress. My God in whom I trust."*

Chapter 17
A Mountain Top Experience that Became a Valley

Principle Learned: *Sometimes we lack the wisdom, experience and humility for a call to greatness. The blessing may be delayed, but it will come! One must accept whatever circumstances you find yourself. Stay positive, change your paradigm and know that God has a specific time, plan and design for you to step into and fulfill your destiny for greatness.*

Scriptural Reference: *Jeremiah 29:11 "For I know the plans I have for you," declares the LORD, plans to prosper you and not to harm you, plans to give you hope."*

Chapter 18
Speaking Words that Landed me in Africa

Principle Learned: *Words you speak have power - when you share positivity about yourself in the universe, it gives you back what you say. And, always be generous and kind to those you meet for you might entertain an angel of help unawares.*

__Scriptural References:__ Proverbs 18:21 "The tongue can bring death or life; those who love to talk will reap the consequences." Hebrews 13:2 "Be not forgetful to entertain strangers: for thereby some have entertained angels unawares."

Chapter 19
My Journey to the Continent of Africa

__Principle Learned:__ Oftentimes, success happens when you give into it and when you make yourself available and open to opportunities. You must be willing to do whatever it takes to pursue it without a promise of success, money, or any expectation whatsoever. My journey to Africa taught me humility, extraordinary faith and the opportunity to change lives in a major way, by sharing my experiences, my faith, and teaching the Word of God using practical and creative ways to impart it.

__Scriptural Reference:__ Colossians 3:23-24 "Whatever you do, work at it with all your heart, as working for the Lord, not for human masters, since you know that you will receive an inheritance from the Lord as a reward. It is the Lord Christ you are serving."

Chapter 20
Stepping into my Destiny

Principle Learned: *People come into your life for a reason and a season. We have the freedom of choice. No one makes you do anything. No, you choose. Serving God is a choice. He does not force you to love Him. He does not force you to serve him. My choice was to serve Him and in doing so, I stepped into my destiny!*

Scriptural Reference: *Psalm 16:5 "The Lord is my inheritance and my cup. You are the one who determines my destiny."*

RESOURCES

Available now on Amazon, Barnes & Nobles, and in the Google Play store (download Dr. Barbara Young's app) and other bookstores.

COMING SOON!

EBook and Audio Book of **"Dancing on Broken Legs: Journey of a D.I.V.A."**

NEW BOOKS COMING (Late 2017)

"Recipes for Personal Best Success: Food for Life"

(Words of encouragement and strategies for individuals to live their best lives)

"Mirror Self Therapy" (MST)

(A fourteen-day intervention coaching program that will transform individual's lives for maximum performance—Use for teenagers and adults)

"High Heels Stepping into the Arms of God"

(The second part of my journey details the spiritual aspects and the many miracles I experienced in my travels around the globe)

Order on website:

www.transformationforsuccess.com/
dancingonbrokenlegs

Email:

info@transformationforsuccess.com

CPSIA information can be obtained
at www.ICGtesting.com
Printed in the USA
LVOW10s1048120617
537803LV00001B/1/P